BETWEEN FAILURE AND SUCCESS

In today's great corporate structures, the young executive who moves ahead must have more than an elementary knowledge of the customs, formalities, and accepted practices of his company, its people and its problems. To stand out and be counted, he must have a most important attribute: executive tact and adroitness in all the many situations to which he will be exposed and in which he will be judged.

He has to know the difference between being strong and being impertinent, between showing respect and being servile. He has to know the unwritten, unspoken code of behavior of the business world. He has to know what his superiors and subordinates expect of him in every interpersonal situation, and has to respond instantly and correctly to every kind of social testing. That is why, whether he knows it or not, he needs—

CORPORATE ETIQUETTE

ABOUT THE AUTHOR: Dr. Milla Alihan is perhaps the first woman to head a firm of industrial psychological and sociological consultants. She has worked with many major corporations and universities, has lectured widely, and is author of *Social Ecology*, considered a classic in its field.

CORPORATE ETIQUETTE

Milla Alihan, Ph. D.

WITH A FOREWORD BY
Franklin M. Jarman

A MENTOR BOOK
NEW AMERICAN LIBRARY
NEW YORK AND SCARBOROUGH, ONTARIO

Library of Congress Catalog Card Number: 72-90404

This is an authorized reprint of a hardcover edition
published by Weybright and Talley, Inc. The hardcover
edition was published simultaneously in Canada by
Clarke, Irwin & Company Limited, Toronto and Vancouver.

MENTOR TRADEMARK REG. U.S. PAT. OFF. AND FOREIGN COUNTRIES
REGISTERED TRADEMARK—MARCA REGISTRADA
HECHO EN CHICAGO, U.S.A.

SIGNET, SIGNET CLASSIC, MENTOR, PLUME, MERIDIAN AND NAL BOOKS
are published in the United States by
New American Library,
1633 Broadway, New York, New York 10019,
in Canada by New American Library of Canada Limited,
81 Mack Avenue, Scarborough, Ontario M1L 1M8

FIRST PRINTING, JULY, 1974

5 6 7 8 9 10 11 12 13

Printed in Canada

To my young clients—
today's executives and tomorrow's presidents

Contents

Foreword

More than at any other time in recent business and industrial history we need to reexamine our values and our judgments. This is the time of change in technology, in outlook, in relationships. But whatever the change in all other facets of life, there is one that remains constant—man's humanity to man. In the business world of today, consideration of others, courtesies, and the give-and-take between men are more vital than ever before. With the social rebellion all around us, we in the business and industrial world must carry forward the sense of continuity and strength. The way of living together, the way of presenting ourselves to each other, the thoughtfulness of others, the use of a common language—these are the topics presented in this book.

Corporate Etiquette is unique, in that here for the first time one can learn to vie properly with the computer, tread lightly the tightropes of yachtsmanship, master the art of keeping the air clear in a company plane, make the most of the Picturephone, and more. . . . Almost every situation a young manager would expect to encounter is covered, except the gravitational aspects of etiquette on the moon, which undoubtedly will appear in a later revision when the experiences there can be tested and verified.

The book is timely, it is pertinent and it will serve as a direction indicator to the young executive of today, and of tomorrow. Picturephone is still in the experimental stage, but very soon it will be a reality to conjure with. Company planes are increasing rapidly, and the computer is here to stay.

Unlike a few decades ago, today demands that the young executive mingle with people, not only within the confines of business, but out in the open, over networks and airwaves, from platforms and at closed-circuit TV conferences. He must understand the message of the computer, but he must also be a thoughtful host, a pleasant guest and, at all times, a goodwill ambassador of his corporation.

Although this book is addressed to the young executive—young both in years and in experience—the senior executives will find many pages of absorbing interest. The executive who is eager to chart a course relatively free from obstructions and hindrances will do well to heed the advice given by Dr. Milla Alihan. As chief executive of a major United States corporation, I am well aware of the important role of corporate etiquette toward achieving sound human relations, not only in the large corporation but also in the smaller business, in whatever part of the country, and in the entire world, for that matter.

Even though the book deals with the "how-to," its basic premise is the kind of mental attitude and philosophy which does not allow the courtesies and the considerations to be empty gestures, but are based upon the most important ingredient of all—sincerity. It is this sincerity, together with the knowledge of the rules of the game, that will clear the young executive's road ahead. I must say that the author treats the subject of corporate etiquette with sophistication and depth. Her years within the walls of a great many industrial and business corporations have given her insights needed for the treatment of the subject.

Dr. Alihan is an industrial psychologist whom I have known for a number of years and with whose work I am well acquainted. She is highly qualified to give counsel to executives, young and old, in their quest of career success. She and her organization have attained high scores in helping widely diversified companies in such fields as engineering, aviation, management consulting, construction, and, of course, soft goods and fashion, which are my own fields. Thus, she has been able to draw on her wide experience to give the executive the benefit of her knowledge.

This book is for the executive whose dreams are not bound down to mundane paths, but who is eager to go up the gratifying escalator of managerial success. I sincerely recommend *Corporate Etiquette* to all executives who would take the one big step of leadership for profits, for growth, and for self-development.

FRANKLIN M. JARMAN
Chairman, Genesco Inc.

Acknowledgments

To acknowledge a debt is not to pay it, but it is half way to settling it. I therefore happily acknowledge the interest, enthusiasm and unstinting cooperation of Morris L. Ernst, Hilda Kassell, M. Kimberlin McGoldrick, Bette Benfield, and Gerhard von Koschembahr.

1. The Young Executive Between Two Worlds

This book is addressed to the young executive straddling two cultures: on the one hand, the business confines permeated by the traditional, conservative standards sustained and often generated by the Establishment; and, on the other, the explosive, high-geared, contagious turmoil of today's youth in action.

Every generation has deplored the rebellious spirit and bad manners of its youth. This has been the platitude enjoyed by the older generation, and the older its members, the wilder the younger generation appears. But our youth today has taken a giant leap away from yesterday. Alarmists regard the rising generation as a falling one. They see the deviating youth as pulling down the very pillars that uphold our civilization.

Yet, however wide the rift between the generations, however deep the ferment of today's revolution, the Establishment still rules the roost, still holds the purse strings, and, certainly, still sets the life pattern of the community. And the Establishment is anchored in business, the corporate body that is the last stronghold of conservatism.

But here, too, innovation has put a dent in the traditional armor of business relations and proprieties. In our increasingly complex world of new technologies, new methods of organizational growth, new requirements of professionalism in business, and new procedures in conducting business, there is much new ground to cover in day-to-day contacts. There are new languages, new managerial techniques, and new gradations of management hierarchy brought about by the rapidly

1

fragmenting specialization in fields only recently developed. Data processing, nuclear physics, systems management, and numerous other innovations have led to unprecedented changes in the status of many individuals in management, separating the old from the new and often blurring the distinctions between timeworn ranks. Such innovations are reshaping business patterns of attitudes and behavior, carrying with them new protocol and new modes of conduct.

In spite of this, mutual consideration and the rules of courteous conduct remain as important today as they were in the eighteenth century when Boswell quoted Dr. Johnson: "Everyone of any education would rather be called a rascal than accused of deficiency in the graces."

In the business environment, the young executive is on the way up, and it befits him in his professional capacity to adhere to corporate requirements, no matter what his leanings and personal style may be.

The young executive may be permissive in his private philosophy: psychedelic art and "literary pornography" may be his bag, and he may even indulge himself in an occasional freak-out or a pot binge, but he must never forget that business has no tolerance for social rebellion. Even the church has a deeper involvement in the youth revolution than do business and industry.

Business represented by top management is strictly conventional with a hard-core determination to maintain the standards of customary amenities. Here one rarely lowers one's guard or flaunts the new breed's mannerisms, attire, or vocabulary. No matter what his personal leanings may be, so long as the young executive is on this side of the business fence, he has to conform, he has to accept the values and ways that business and industry prescribe for members of management.

There is unwritten corporate etiquette to which the average successful executive adheres most of the time. There are rules of business behavior as there are rules of social conduct. These rules help make business relations easier, pleasanter, and certainly more profitable. When Georges Clemenceau's secretary complained about diplomatic folderol, saying that it is nothing but a lot of hot air, the famous Tiger of France retorted, "All etiquette is hot air, but that's what is in our automobile tires, and see how it eases the bumps!"

You undoubtedly have basic knowledge of customs, formalities, and accepted practices of the business world.

You probably know most of them, but no matter how broad your know-how, there are new business situations, as well as situations to which you have not yet been exposed. These will surely come your way as you progress in your career.

Even in the most familiar situations one can benefit substantially by reexamining one's manners and one's conduct and by bringing up to date some of the thought-and-action habits formed over the years.

The average executive may follow correct style instinctively, but there are many situations with which instinct does not seem to be concerned. And, remember, there is really no one who will tell the executive what impression he conveys by his manner, how acceptable his manners are, and whether some of his mannerisms are an asset or a liability to him.

Self-examination and self-awareness can help, but to have this kind of objective self-insight, one needs a guide, a "direction indicator." This book is designed to serve as just such an indicator and as an aid to awareness of one's ways and one's actions. This is not a treatise on elementary etiquette, it is rather a tie-in of civilities and good manners with good business and success in a career.

WHO IS THIS MAN?

"The young executive" is an ambitious, hard-working, persevering, and thoroughly involved individual who has joined the managerial ranks of a corporation and whose title conveys the magic of executive status. Possibly, he is one of the bright, able, and promising individuals who was tagged for the job while he was still a senior at a university or in one of the major schools of business administration. He was the object of the intensive manhunt for executive material on the campuses—the stampede for talent which has proliferated into major programs in corporate personnel departments and executive recruiting firms. From the start, our young man was aware that management recognized his potential. He came armed with a diploma and a long string of points in business courses. He was young enough to have kept his self-confidence intact. He was bolstered by the knowledge that he had the intelligence, the capabilities, and the professional training to meet the inevitable challenge and responsibilities within the corporation's criteria of success.

He applied himself diligently, he learned fast, and he never lost the thread of his ambition. Yet, for the time being he rates only a desk in the general office, or a glass-partitioned cubicle. One wag defined a junior executive as "anyone who works in an office sitting down." But his sights are set for the wall-to-wall-carpeted office with the ego-satisfying title on the door, and a salary check showing commensurate ciphers—his ultimate reward.

Our young man may have flouted his social consciousness with vigor and sincerity while he was a student in college, but now his career image must be tailored to meet the corporate pattern. As a member of the corporate family, he has a responsibility to present a façade that will be a credit to the organization as well as to himself. As a member of management he becomes versed in the rules of corporate etiquette and tacitly agrees to put them into practice.

THE CORPORATE FAMILY

A corporation is a highly complex, stratified, and often hazardous maze. Yet, it is essentially an assemblage of persons who have to conduct themselves with civility and understanding; otherwise, the work environment becomes untenable. Basically, a corporation is a society of individuals with common goals, interests, and attitudes, who must work together as a team in a congenial, amiable atmosphere to keep the machinery of the organization running smoothly.

By observing the rules of courteous behavior within its corporate family, a company has a controlled, efficient work force which reflects itself in its dealings with the public. Moreover, it is an elementary business truism that it pays to be courteous. Courtesy is a profitable asset in any undertaking.

To function harmoniously and efficiently, the corporate body, or, for that matter, any group, must follow the basic concepts of civility, courtesy, and consideration. It is the give-and-take between individuals that is important. The young executive's role is to show an aptitude to please, a readiness to respond, and a willingness to accommodate himself to the working philosophy of the organization. Living by the golden rule and operating on the principle of intelligent trust can unlock for the young tyro many executive doors.

Generally, the managerial hierarchy establishes the climate and sets the tone. From there, through the chain of command, the organizational life style sifts down to all levels of the corporate structure.

No two organizations operate within exactly the same framework. In addition to the standard rules of expected conduct, each organization has its own unwritten rules of corporate etiquette, where position and rank are given their due. Even in the most democratic organization, which may appear to have no hierarchial strata between executives, there is, nontheless, a finely graded system where the prerogatives of bossdom prevail. Status may be understated, with seemingly casual acceptance, but no individual with his wits about him should confuse informality with presumptive conduct.

A top position, attained by brain sweat, hard work, and fractured nerves, is a costly achievement. Yet, unless the aspirant wraps his efforts in actions and words that elicit approval, his victory is hollow. Cloaked in good manners, the effort of an aspiring executive can be rewarded tenfold. Propriety and courtesy are the mainstay of profit-bearing relationships.

THE JET AGE AND THE ESTABLISHMENT

Job etiquette differs from social etiquette in that position and rank on the job are more clearly defined and require fuller recognition. But the traditional conventions, the amenities, the basic decencies of a civilized society, are as applicable to the business environment as they are to the social scene.

Every executive is charged with the responsibility of setting the pattern for tact and polite conduct. The man whose posture is servile in the presence of his superiors and rude or offhand with his subordinates has forgotten the old chestnut "Be nice to the little man on your way up, you might meet him on your way down."

In the job environment, it is the junior executive who is most vulnerable. He may be in his late twenties or early thirties, with two to ten years' business experience. In corporate parlance he remains the young executive until his performance is recognized and he has earned for himself a promotion with a meaningful title.

Our present-day young executive is caught in an ambivalent trap. As a product of the jet age, he is pulled into the quicksand of the new far-out philosophy and life style. But, at the same time, he must harness his tempo to keep pace with the traditional way set by the old guard. The young executive must accept the fact that he is a member of the business community. If he has the ambition and drive to make the grade, he will be mindful of the sometimes discredited term "conform" as part of his working equipment.

The new life style of the "now" generation, who believe in doing their own thing, almost ended in disaster for one young executive in a utility company. A promising young man with proven executive ability, he had a knowledgeable approach toward his work, earned the confidence of his superiors, and in every way conducted himself with propriety. It was not long before he received a new nameplate on his desk which read "Assistant Manager." There was a comparable increase in salary.

His wife decided the promotion called for a celebration. In addition to personal friends, several of the young man's business associates were invited to the cocktail party at the young couple's home.

The host greeted his guests in a white turtleneck sweater and a noisy plaid blazer; his wife was dressed in a flamboyant pants suit ablaze with junk jewelry. Their personal friends were also costumed in what could only be described as "hip haute couture." The business associates in their conventional three-button sack suits felt quite out of place and uncomfortable.

The next day the corridors of the organization echoed with rumors that the young couple were swingers, their friends psychedelic, and that the party was a "bash." The young man became acutely aware that his superiors were beginning to regard him with suspicion, and his peers treated him with the kind of amusing indulgence that does not inspire confidence. This was an expensive lesson for the young executive.

Even at a strictly social occasion, if business associates are present, it is wiser to conform to the conventions of the Establishment. Whether he is aware of it or not, the young executive is under constant surveillance; every action, every mannerism, his speech, his tactics—all these will determine whether he measures up to executive material. He is judged not only by the cut of his clothes but by the cut of his mind and the cut of his manners.

WHO ARE THE EXECUTIVES?

Top and middle management executives are the backbone of American business and industry. They are the decision-makers. Their business know-how is indicated by their titles. They are unique products of the twentieth century, with a real stake in the economy of the country. They are charged with a trusteeship that may affect not only the profits and the growth of their own company but also the Dow Jones industrial averages. Their managerial experience and talents are steered toward the ultimate goal which, in the lexicon of business terminology, is simplified into reduced production costs, increased sales, and booming profits.

There are almost as many definitions of an executive as there are men who merit the title. A composite picture of an executive is provided by the president of a large company: "An 'executive' is a relatively high-level member of the management family whose work is largely in the area of decision-making and policy formulation. His capacity is such that his judgment, perception, and skill in properly delegating responsibility will weigh heavily on the long-term success or failure of the business."

A very important and rather new ingredient in the definition of an executive is a high "human relations quotient." Within the last couple of decades, business and industry have placed more and more emphasis on the ability of an executive to get along with his subordinates, his peers, and his superiors.

Good human relations are a sign of good management. The trend today is toward stronger group cohesiveness and group interaction. Human relations in this sense emphasize mutual respect for each other's worth. It is the managerial state in which human and democratic values are interrelated.

One executive recruiter estimates that nine out of ten clients stipulate, as their number-one requirement for a managerial post, the ability "to get along with people." He had a client who was more specific. He gave an outline of what he expected from his incoming executives in terms of human relations: "I don't want a hatchet man. I want a man who knows the difference between persuasion and coercion. I not only want but need a man who doesn't feel so threatened that he won't recognize and encourage executive potential in a trainee. Our company is growing, and we need all the executive talent we can get."

There are no obvious yardsticks to measure human relations. The very fact that human relations have become the prime factor in executive training programs is an acknowledgment that organizational machinery is manufacturing new signposts for its executives: "Handle with Care." The old Hollywood stereotype of Mr. Big barking orders at cringing executives, or the myths circulating about the outrageous behavior in big companies, are no longer acceptable organizational portraits.

In his book, *My Forty Years with Ford*, Charles E. Sorensen relates: "Someone was always spreading stories about how hard and tough I was. . . . One story with more lives than a cat is that I kicked a box from under a sitting Detroit Edison repairman, believing him to be a Ford employee who should be standing up at his work, and that the Edison man got up and knocked me flat. For more than ten years I have had a standing offer of $1,000 to anyone able to prove that story true. Another $1,000 offer holds good for anyone able to prove that Harry Bennett, Ford's superpoliceman and pistol-packing errand boy, got Ford to fire me in 1944. My money is safe; neither $1,000 offer will ever be claimed successfully."

If there are any misinterpretations of why Charles Sorensen was called "Cast-Iron Charlie," the explanation is simple. It was Henry Ford who gave him that name when the Model T was still a gleam in Mr. Ford's mind. The need to produce better high-grade castings for a low-priced, mass-produced car inspired Mr. Sorensen to experiment with gray iron. The nickname stuck, but had no relevance to Mr. Ford's habit of saying, "Let Charlie do it," whenever a disagreeable job was called for.

BRIDGING THE EXECUTIVE GAP

The Older Executive's Dilemma in Training a Younger Man

A significant executive function emphasized in a study conducted by *Fortune Magazine* was "to maintain and develop an organization of trained subordinates to achieve the company's objectives."

The older executive is expected to encourage and help in the development of the younger executive through instruction, through guidance, and through example. As one general manager of GM's Buick Division said: "I just tell a man I can't promote him unless he's got an assistant ready to take his place. Then he relaxes and delegates."

Contrary to the myths and horror stories that become enlarged and more horrendous as they make the rounds, there are senior executives who project the father image in their dealings with their subordinates, grooming and encouraging them for promotion with rewarding salary increases. Nevertheless, it is precisely in this area of training a younger man where the middle-aged executive, who doubtless still shows scars of his battles to achieve his present position, demonstrates his ability to face up to the test of positive human relations.

Training a younger man with the thought that one day he may take over some of his boss's responsibilities is a planned relinquishment of authority not easy for an older man to accept. There are executives who are haunted by the bugaboo that there is as much danger from those who work under them as from those who work with them. The younger executive has to learn to understand that this is not a personal reflection on him, but merely that the older man's insecurity is showing. Guidance by a superior with these drawbacks is a tough assignment for an executive trainee. His first course is to learn how to win his superior's confidence.

The Greater the Man, the Greater the Courtesy

Courtesy under all circumstances, even when the tensions seem unendurable, should be the young executive's number-one guideline. This does not mean that he has to be servile or fawning. Far from it. It is simply that he must keep his resentments on a leash, his temper under control and show a willingness to work hard and do his level best at whatever his superior assigns to him, without stepping out of line. A sign of appreciation to the boss also helps: a show of interest, for example, when the boss projects a good idea; a readiness to participate when coping with prickly problems. As the head of a management consulting firm puts it, "Whenever possible, be gracious without being ingratiating, and be pleasant without being subservient."

The boss is a human being with human frailties and human responses. A kind word, a tactful show of thoughtfulness, might mellow him to the point of making him forget his role of curmudgeon. The young executive might keep in his mental file the thought that when *he* becomes a supervisory executive he, too, will welcome a word of appreciation from his subordinates.

In a broader sense junior executives are Xeroxed copies of their superiors. They have to be tuned in to the same channel, and they have to direct their thinking toward the same goals. To a degree, young aspirants have to temper their opinions and direct their actions to coincide with those of their superiors, who, in turn, make an effort to reflect the company policies. It is teamwork in action in which the very word "company" is translated into a cohesive pattern of working together.

A meeting of minds is an essential part of the game directed toward achieving a smooth working relationship. The other important ingredient is courtesy with tact. Courtesy is the passport that will open the portals of success wider for the junior executive who, for the time being, has only a toe-hold in the doorway.

A case in point is the time when Victor Davies, a young cost accountant, was sent by his home office to Pennsylvania to sparkplug the latetest acquisition, a $7-million metal-works factory with a comatose graph. As young Davies described it: "I was led to believe that it was run by some old fogie know-nothings who never got around to learning the significance of data processing and systems management. They thought technology was an expensive word, not in their class."

Davies continued: "I was feeling really great. I was going down to Pennsylvania to prove that management knew what they were doing when they singled me out as their fair-haired boy. I had the ball and I was running for a touchdown and wasn't going to brook any interference. Sure, I made a thorough analysis of the factory records—their past performance, production facilities, inventory control, and all that jazz. Then I worked out what I knew was a dynamic program, and was all set for a blockbusting job."

His first meeting was with the man who had founded, headed, and built up the company a quarter of a century ago and who had been retained as president by the new parent body. A gentleman of the old school with courtly manners, he took all the thunder out of Davies' approach. As Davies related, "I expected to be treated like an interloper. In fact, I was warned I would be by some of the more experienced men in the home office. I was all primed for a battle with no holds barred. But when I met the president, I was completely disarmed. He got up to greet me when I entered his office, gave me a warm handshake as though he were genuinely glad I came; he offered me a chair and a cigar, and suggested that I might like to relax first, after my trip. He was so polite I had to return the compliment.

"He told me that he had arranged for me to meet his managers at lunch that day at his club, and as he explained it, 'so that you may get to know them, and they get to know you, under the most favorable circumstances.' And how right he was! These men turned out to be as polite and as cordial as the chief, and we got off to a good friendly start. Natch, I got the message and toned down my approach. I played their game.

"Of course, as the work progressed, we got into tight corners. Many of them. But it was all low-keyed, and I learned there and then that there is a vast difference between arguing a point and discussing a problem.

"My greatest difficulty was with the chief. He was polite, but skeptical, and resistant to drastic changes. I had to learn to be patient, explain over and over again how the new control systems I was recommending would benefit his production. There were times when I thought I would lose my temper. But I managed to control my impatience. I was careful not to make the chief feel that he was old hat, and that I knew more than he did. We discussed each point like reasonable men. Sometimes I'd give in a little, sometimes he would, until we reached an acceptable compromise. I didn't achieve everything I set out to do that first round, but we did make some headway. Subsequently, when the chief began to understand the new systems and how they worked, he went all out for them. It took eight months, but it was worth the effort.

"Never during those eight months did I see the chief ruffled or impatient. He'd hear me out without interrupting. When I finished, he'd start a long-winded explanation of why he didn't think this or that was feasible. Believe me, it took some doing for me to hold my tongue and wait until *he* had his say.

"The boys in the home office kidded the shirt off me about being a super eagle Boy Scout, because the chief always referred to me as 'that polite young man, Victor Davies.' They aren't being so witty now, since they found out that the chief has asked our top management if they would release me to become his executive vice-president."

Victor Davies understood and was quick to respond to true courtesy. It was not only his external conduct of polite conventional behavior, but he had that extra plus, *intuitive situational judgment*. He had the sensitivity to recognize and the wisdom to understand the character of the man he was dealing with, and he related accordingly.

2. Manners at Work

THE SLIPPERY LADDER

Good manners are not the sole attributes for executive promotion, but knowing what is proper at the right time and place is a boost upward on the slippery ladder of success. There is no guarantee that good manners alone will escalate a young hopeful to become chairman of the board; but a business career can suffer unless one masters the art of courtesy.

For more than three years Arthur L. had been working in the industrial plastic manufacturing plant of a multimillion-dollar diversified corporation. A decentralization program precipitated several attractive openings on managerial levels. Arthur L. was confident that he was slated to head the production department of one of the divisions. His interest in the work, his educational background, his technical knowledge and skills, and his job performance, all added up to his eligibility. When an executive from another plant was transferred and given the job, Arthur L. was in a state of shock.

He stormed into the vice-president's office and demanded: "Why was I passed over? Why didn't I get the job?"

"Sit down, Arthur. This is not a convenient time for me to talk to you, but so long as you're here we may as well get this off our chests."

Arthur slumped into a chair. "Look at my job record," he insisted. "When I gave my progress report at the last divisional meeting, I got a tremendous hand."

"True," the VP agreed. "No complaints about your job performance. You've got the technical know-how, you've shown initiative and drive, and we're not unaware that you've put in a hell of a lot of overtime work. But, my lad, you've got a problem, and I'm going to give it to you straight. You've got a case of social halitosis, and it doesn't look good for the executive image."

"What do you mean? I don't get you."

"Your manners, my lad. Your manners. Look at you now, slouching in your chair. You sit that way in the conference room, too. Sit up, for Pete's sake. Now here's another thing. You barged into my office without inquiring from my secretary or buzzing me first to find out if it was convenient for me to see you. As a matter of fact, it's damned inconvenient. I've got a rush report to get out and, for all you know, I might have been in conference, or I might—"

"Your door was open and I saw you were alone."

"You are interrupting me, Arthur. You did the same thing to Don when he was giving his report at the meeting. You seem to have forgotten that Don outranks you. And talking about the meeting, that was no place for you to start a knock-down, drag-out argument with Fred, especially when B.J. was in the chair. It's true you had the facts, and Fred got lost in the shuffle, but it sounded like a fishmonger's brawl, and if you think for one minute that by downgrading Fred you were impressing B.J., you've got another think coming. Management takes a dim view of an executive who doesn't know how to behave like one. All this may sound trivial to you, but you are a representative of the company inside the plant as well as outside. Your actions, good or bad, reflect on the company. Now I can go on and tell you more."

"No, thanks. I've heard enough." Arthur L. stalked out of the office and out of the company.

THE FIRST IMPORTANT DECISION

You are a young executive. You have served your apprenticeship as a member of the managerial group long enough to evaluate yourself. You occupy a position on the rising slopes of the corporation. Your exact rank may not be clearly defined as yet, but the direction of your career is indicated.

This is the time for you to call a meeting with yourself and make your decision—your first important decision-making test on a long-range program. Your agenda should include the following questions:

(1) Have I the qualifications and guts for executive responsibility?

(2) Do I regard my present position merely as a job, or has it got the potential for career development?

(3) Is this the organization I want to be identified with?

(4) Is my boss with me or against me?

(5) Are my associates the kind of people with whom I am prepared to spend the best part of my life?

Your conclusions must be decisive. You live half of your life on your job; your livelihood depends upon it; even your personality, character, and life style are molded by your work environment.

Your first loyalty is to yourself. As master of your own destiny you are in full control. Only when you face yourself realistically will you be able to estimate your personal worth, act with authority, and relate to your associates with a sense of security.

If you feel you are at a dead end in your job, this is the time to make the move.

JOB MOBILITY

Previously referred to as job-hopping, job mobility is another fractured symptom of organizational life, whereby the young executive is called upon to make a serious self-evaluation. At one time job-hopping, reflected by one's resume, was regarded as a negative recommendation. Today the picture is changed. The market value for proven executive ability and intelligence is rated high. A young man who is a "comer" is expected to be a "mover."

Job counselors and personnel managers know that companies have no compunction about raiding rival organizations by luring their promising young men away with offers of better pay, higher status, and added fringe benefits. A man in his late twenties or early thirties can afford to postpone thoughts about retirement benefits and pension plans until he finds his proper niche. But better pay and higher status are something else.

YOU AND YOUR DIRECT SUPERIOR

Your boss may not be your idea of the type of man you would like to work for. But unless you go elsewhere, you have no choice. You have to accept the inevitable with good grace. Under all circumstances you must remember that you have to work *with* him and not *against* him. It's like a shotgun marriage, and the junior executive has to make most of the concessions.

Here are a few clues to help you:

(1) Wait for your boss to establish your working relationship, be it formal, informal, or friendly. He may call you by your first name, but the straw in his stuffed shirt may get ruffled if you address him by his first name or use his initials, until he suggests it himself.

(2) Keep your boss informed. Send him carbon copies of important letters, memos, and proposals. This will have two advantages for you:

    a. It will clue in your superior as to your thinking process and working procedures, since your progress and advancement depend to a large degree on his judgment of you.

    b. He will be updated on all matters relating to his department. You won't embarrass him, or put him in the untenable position of keeping him in ignorance about matters that directly concern him. Always remember that you are a team, working in unison, and that his job is as important to him as yours is to you.

(3) Consult your direct superior before making any departmental and/or corporate commitments.

(4) Respect your boss's working time. Don't interrupt him with constant questions. He has knotty business problems of his own to cope with. Make a list of the points to be discussed, and then meet with him when time permits. Or send him a memo. A busy executive often prefers that. He can then deal with the subject at his convenience, giving the matter the attention it deserves.

(5) Observe the chain of command. Never go over your boss's head. This is both bad business tactics and bad business

manners. If you and he reach an impasse, especially on a problem exceptionally critical from your point of view, ask your boss's permission to have someone higher up arbitrate the question. If your boss agrees, send a memo, and be sure he gets a carbon copy and that the higher-up understands that this is a joint request.

(6) If your supervisor criticizes you for a mistake you've made, don't take it personally, however rough he may be about it. It isn't easy for anyone to be critical and at the same time gracious. Just remember that he is not criticizing you as a person as much as he is concerned with keeping the machinery of his department running smoothly. Try to take his advice on how to correct the mistake and how to prevent it from occurring in the future, and you'll both avoid unnecessary friction.

(7) If the criticism is unjustified, swallow your indignation. Try not to blurt out that "it was Mike's fault." You'll only start a chain reaction with Mike polishing his stiletto. Blame-shifting will reflect unfavorably on your character in your boss's judgment; he may mark you as a troublemaker and as someone unequipped to accept responsibility.

(8) You may disagree with your supervisor on certain issues. If he does not accept your recommendations, don't harp on the subject. There are certain individuals who constitutionally regard as wrong another person's way of handling a problem simply because it hasn't been their way of dealing with it.

(9) Your personal life is your private affair. Your boss's office is not a confessional. It is neither his nor the company's concern that you are having trouble with your mother-in-law, that your wife wants a new fur coat, or that you need more money. Even when you are in a nonworking situation with your boss or any member of the firm, you should never, never, take your soul out for an airing.

YOU AND YOUR PEERS

The corporate pyramid has a broad, solid base of the lower-echelon work force that tapers upward, gradually accommodating the various executive levels, until it reaches the slim finial that has room at the top for only a highly selected few.

In the center of the pyramid swarm the different-ranking executives jockeying for position, trying, if not to reach the finial, at least to gain a foothold on the upper reaches. The competition may be undeclared, but it is keen, elbows are sharp and sabotage is not an unknown factor. In many corporations the competition among executives can be more intense than the competition that ought to be exerted against rival companies.

This corporate malaise afflicts all companies, wasting much valuable executive brain power and diverting productive management skills into the effort to survive in what has come to be known as the executive jungle. These undercurrents may not always appear on the surface. Outwardly most executives are sufficiently sophisticated and urbane to behave politely, with seeming consideration.

Since there is little room at the top, there are more trainees and junior executives than there are slots for them in the higher ranks. The competition on this level is also keen. The young executive has much at stake. He is in the prime of his career. Will his intelligence and industry establish a firm career base, or will he be one of the dropouts?

It is for the upcoming executive to decide which road he wants to pursue: the hostility-anxiety-ridden one of intrigue, wearing his self-made straitjacket, or the road where human values are still held in high esteem and where he is master of his own soul and his conscience. His road may prove either an escalator or a treadmill. How far he gets up the corporate line of succession depends on him.

The success mystique is fraught with many unpredictables, but the old reliables of job performance, proven loyalty to the company, ability to communicate with fellow workers, and agreeable manners still get high priority in executive evaluation by top management. Steer clear of the dogfights as best you can. They can prove destructive to your own morable, inducing tension and anxiety, as well as undermining your job status and security. Use your energies constructively; build toward goodwill and amicable communication with your fellow workers.

THE JUNIOR EXECUTIVE AND
THE HERD INSTINCT

As comtemporaries who speak the same language of ambition, hope, and despair, young executives instinctively herd together. They have much in common. Rivalries are kept under wraps. Their business and personal problems have a relative similarity. The dogmatic know-nothingness of the old guard, the eccentricities of superiors, the mortgage on the house, the new car, and the clever thing Junior said yesterday are all contributing factors to engendering a hospitable environment. Young executives lunch together not only because of the organizational stigma that an executive who lunches by himself is an oddball but also for companionship.

It is inevitable that in some instances mutual understanding and common interests will blossom into friendship. The competitive hatchet will be left unsharpened, and man's natural desire for harmonious coexistence will take over. But business friendships, like those made on ocean voyages, are usually intense, intimate, and quickly forgotten once the individuals have gone their separate ways.

Relating to your peers with whom you have intellectual and common interests may be easy and relaxed, but there are still pitfalls. Here are some experience-proven guidelines a wise young executive should keep in mind.

(1) Be friendly but not intimate. Too deep a personal involvement in business makes it difficult to maintain an objective attitude. Moreover, an intimate knowledge about yourself and your private affairs may turn into a weapon in the hands of an overambitious, unscrupulous, or scandal-mongering associate.

(2) Don't encourage intimate confidences on the part of a fellow worker. His problems may impose a personal obligation upon you which may affect your rational judgment in a crisis situation. If he reveals too many confidential details about himself, you are bound to become personally involved and you will lose your objectivity.

(3) You may have the gift of mimicry and like to show off your talents before an appreciative audience. If any of your associates are present, whether the occasion is a working or a nonworking one, never use any of the executives or

other sacred cows of the organization as your subjects. Word is sure to get around, and no-nonsense executives would take a dim view when they learn that they have been the butt of your humor, however innocent or clever.

(4) Under the guise of friendship, an associate may ask you a business question that is improper. Don't brush him off with indignation. Be noncommittal and as nonchalantly courteous as you can. He has been indiscreet and tactless, but you need not follow suit.

(5) An associate may ask you for material from your files that you are not sure he ought to have. Find some excuse. Tell him your superior has the folder, or that your secretary is in the midst of doing something urgent and you cannot disturb her. Stall him until you can query your boss as to whether it is okay for you to give him the information he wants.

(6) On the other hand, if a high-ranking executive asks you for material when your superior is not available, you may have no alternative other than to give it to him without delay. But be sure you tell your superior about it when he returns.

(7) You may on occasion have to work on confidential reports, or keep restricted information on your desk. Keep these papers in a folder in the event an associate or an unexpected visitor comes into your office. It would be the natural thing for you to close the folder without appearing to be rude.

(8) You and your associates may be in the habit of having lunch together. Should you be fortunate enough to be promoted ahead of the others, appear to take it in your stride without bursting your shirt buttons in front of your associates. You will have to walk a tightrope to maintain the friendship of your associates without seeming to patronize them. You never know when your executive levels may coincide again, or collide. In the meantime, with your new exalted position, there will be some changes in your relationships. These changes should take place gradually; there should be an evolution rather than a revolution in your attitude toward your former associates.

It might be a good idea for you to arrange to give them a "celebration" luncheon. If they give you a celebration treat, you go ahead with your plans anyhow. In a way, it is your friendly gesture of farewell because in your new position your luncheon commitments will more likely be with individuals of another echelon. Your associates will get the message that it is not your intention to pull rank, but that SOP (standard operating procedure) is breaking the continuity of your quasi-social meetings.

THE FIRST-NAME SYNDROME

The use of first names is causing disapproving shudders among some upholders of the Establishment. But we are confronted with a generation that talks in shorthand, with a vocabulary that is not always compatible with either tradition or conventions.

In some companies, such as advertising agencies, public-relations offices, and other firms in the communications media, where a laissez-faire attitude prevails, everyone from the boss down is known by his first name. Surnames are out; intimacy is in. But many of the major corporations, notably those in finance and industry, adhere to the formalities. Deference to rank is the order of the day. The officers and the executives are called "Mr." The use of the first name is generally frowned upon, and every employee is expected to mind his corporate manners.

A helpful yardstick is that the older and the larger the firm, the more formal. First names are used mainly when signing letters or checks. In the canyons of Wall Street, "Mr." is generally the required form of address. But in other regions, notably in the West and Southwest, the social as well as business interrelationships are more relaxed and informal, and a first-name basis is common.

The younger, smaller corporations are inclined to be less formal. First names, initials, and even nicknames are used all the way up and down the escalator. However, this may be acceptable only in the front office, and not at the plant or mill, where the white collar still gets the deferential nod over the coverall.

Carl Noble, a marketing executive, whose New England background inhibited him from calling anyone by his first name, said he had to "learn by osmosis." The very first day on a new job in a large corporation, his superior addressed him as Carl, just as he referred to the division president as

Harry. This alerted Carl that if he wanted to stay "in" with top management, he had to accept instant intimacy, and play the name game.

You will have to take your own soundings in this confused sea of changing manners to decide what is appropriate in your organizational setup—whom you call by the first name and whom you call "Mr."

OFFICE POLITICS

A Team or a Tug-of-War?

A wit is quoted as saying that "in politics a man usually learns to rise below his principles."

Office politics is a fact of life in every company and at every corporate level. Some companies deliberately encourage the competitive spirit among employees under the impression that competition is a stimulant to bigger and better achievements. In every competitive encounter there is a struggle for supremacy. From every struggle emerges a winner, but as in many lawsuits, one may win the case and still be the loser.

Rivalry in corporations to obtain that next higher-level job is inevitable. There is only one spot available, and many candidates are vying for it. Men of conscience with respect for the Marquis of Queensberry rules will play fair. But there are those who will play "politics" with an amoral disregard for the rules, resorting to trickery, even savage tactics. As Disraeli said: "In politics there is no honor."

The head of a fast-growing plastics corporation is fond of relating this story. When his young son asked him: "Daddy, how did you get to be president of the company?" he replied: "Well, son, while the others were busy slugging it out as to who was to get the job, I just slipped in over the barricades and took over."

Some corporations try to minimize office politics by diverting the competitive spirit into channels that would benefit the company. The incentives are directed toward the sales chart, toward dramatizing the production picture, toward juicy profit earnings. Executive conflicts rarely come out in the open. But even under these conditions, an executive with an eye on the goalpost will brook no interference and will have no compunctions about undermining and even misdirecting and misinforming a possible rival.

Office politics and the machinations of the activist do not always surface and may not always be discernible to the observer. But the underground rumblings can rock the stability and sap the productive energy of a man who does not want to be involved, but who merely wants to do his job.

The admonition to stay out of office politics would be pertinent if it were possible. In the eye of an administrative hurricane even the innocent and the nonparticipants may be caught up in the storm.

The Protective Armor

There are a few protective measures an executive can arm himself with that may not involve him too deeply in the skirmishes:

(1) Establish a quasi-isolationist policy. Be neutral. Listen to everyone but hold your counsel. It is difficult to remain placid in the din and fury. It will take all your controls to "play it cool." Your outward manners should be calm and collected; your attitude toward everyone concerned is that of a friend, not an enemy. Your own inner turmoil may be charged with doubts, even sympathy for one of the participants, but you must remain objective. So long as you do, you'll be able to hold your own.

Adlai Stevenson phrased it succinctly when he said: "To act coolly, intelligently, and prudently in perilous circumstances is the test of a man."

(2) You cannot pretend that office politics does not exist. Against your own will you may become embroiled. If that does happen, stay out in the open. Let the snipers fight it out among themselves, but your position as a neutral noncombatant will dispel any hostility or animosity on the part of the victims caught in the squeeze play. "You cannot be all things to all men," but you can take a neutral though interested stand and be able to look each man in the eye without flinching.

(3) Intrigue is like an octopus whose vicious tentacles suck in even those who struggle to keep clear of the underground plotting and planning. Unwittingly you may be roped into a conspiracy. For example, your boss may be conniving to get a higher job, but in order to do so he may want to discredit

another executive who is also a candidate. Your superior may try to use you as a pawn. He may ask you, possibly in an innocent and offhand manner, to ferret out certain information, casting you in the role of a small-time James Bond. Don't rise up in righteous indignation. You will only earn his animosity. Practice diplomacy, which is the fine art of telling half-truths, or the finer art of telling half-lies. Tell him you will make every effort to get the lowdown for him, and when the proper time comes, confess you have failed in your mission.

(4) Your pacifistic insulation may be shattered by a foul ball out of left field. Suddenly, you find you are the target of a plot. Executive paranoia has many hidden causes. In some organizations executives live dangerously, and the ground rule is survival of the fittest. Don't lose your head and jump into the fray in a rash and mindless way. Take the problem home with you. Think it through. Analyze it. Once you understand your antagonist, you'll understand the cause, and you will be in a better position to seek the cure. In *The Magic Mountain*, Thomas Mann wrote: "Order and simplification are the first steps toward the mastery of a subject—the actual enemy is the unknown."

Warning Signal: Danger Ahead

Executive gamesmanship calls for a cool head, steady nerves, and a polite demeanor to disarm the enemy and to cope with various corporate exigencies.

The surprise attack may come from your superior. Suddenly he is unjustifiably critical, demanding, and generally destructive in his estimation of your work. These are obvious signs that something has happened and that he is gunning for you. Your only defense is to remain calm. Don't panic. Continue to perform your duties as best as you can under the circumstances. Your one safeguard is not to harbor inner doubts about your own ability and not to surrender your self-respect to underhanded counterattacks.

A good example is the story of one young executive who understandably prefers to remain anonymous. He had his boss's confidence and support, when he was suddenly baffled by a complete change in climate. Not only was he getting the deep-freeze treatment but the memos that reached him from his boss's desk were vitriolic enough to take the starch out of him. Everything the young executive did seemed to be wrong, or rather, not the way the boss wanted things done. He spent many anxious days and nights trying to figure out what tribal customs he had violated. The unjustified victimizing continued until the young man decided it was time for a showdown. He asked to see the boss.

At first the older man was rough and uncompromising, but the young executive was determined to keep calm. As he told the story later: "Mr. Barton spoke 'loud but not good.' He threw the book at me and I couldn't figure it out. He kept repeating that all this time he had been grooming me for his job, and here I was letting him down. But he didn't spell it out as to how I was letting him down. The more I let him talk, the more I began to get the pitch. He had been expecting to get the group manager's job in our division. But management transferred another man from the Detroit office, and I guess that threw Mr. Barton for a loop. He had been building me up for *his* job, expecting the promotion, but now that he didn't get it, he panicked. He began to look upon me as a threat. So he started tearing me down. We're working together now on a sort of armed-truce basis, but it isn't as it used to be, and I guess it never will be again."

If the relationship between you and your boss gets much worse, and you find that your working vitality is being drained, you are justified in taking the matter up with a higher authority. Some corporations maintain an open-door policy. When IBM was a much smaller company, Thomas J. Watson introduced such a practice. Any dissatisfied employee who could not get satisfaction at a lower level was invited to visit him personally.

However, an executive should go with his complaints to one higher-up only if:

(1) he knows that he cannot discuss the subject with his superior;

(2) he has spoken to his superior with a view of discovering where the trouble lies and got nowhere;

(3) he has informed his superior of his intentions;

(4) he has invited his superior to be present for a man-to-man confrontation. (This is not mandatory.)

Be wary of an associate who is suddenly free with his tips and inside information. A higher-level job may be in the offing. Your friendly associate may give you the lowdown: "So-and-so was fired because he was introducing too many new ideas into the working plan of his department. Management didn't want these radical changes made. They wanted the department to maintain status quo." He might even be kind enough to let you know that he is telling you this because he knows that you are in line for that job. When you do go for your interview, you feel you are well armed with the right approach. You assure management you will maintain the policies of the department, only to find out later that this is not what management wants and that your friendly tipster who had the inside track got the job himself.

Is someone stealing your thunder? A not uncommon maneuver is for another executive to take credit for something you have done. It is occupational kleptomania where anything is fair game unless you are prudent enough to expedite the action properly tagged with your name.

Henry Small, who is the assistant to the marketing manager for radio and communications equipment, came up with what he thought was a brilliant idea. He had found the solution of how to break the bottleneck in order to get their latest product, still dubbed "P49," off to a good start. He was lunching with Bob Whiting, one of the other assistants in the division, as yet a nonadjectived executive. Henry, in a burst of creative enthusiasm, blurted out the idea to Bob, "to try it out for size, and to get your reaction." Bob, who was an eager-beaver type, working toward that coveted promotion and title, thought the idea was "okay and might work." When Henry got back to his office, he began to figure out how best to present the idea to his supervisor. But before he could put his thoughts on paper, Bob had quickly memoed *his* supervisor, and walked off with the kudos and the credit.

When Henry related this story, he said that he decided not to raise a fuss. It was beneath his dignity to get into a "he-said-I-said" kind of wrangle. Besides, he had a similar problem with his own supervisor. He needed all his creative energies to solve that problem, and he did.

Whenever Henry submitted his progress reports to his boss he saw to it that they were properly filled out with his name, his divisional responsibilities, and always worded "we did" such and such. But, he discovered his supervisor would change the "we" to first personal singular, remove Henry's name, have his secretary retype it, and then submit the report as his own.

Henry's solution was worthy of King Solomon. He continued to write his reports in the nominative plural, but interjected now and then such phrases as "At the instruction of Mr. Dawson" (his supervisor) or "It was Mr. Dawson's idea."

This strategy worked. Thereafter, Mr. Dawson never changed the dot of an *i*, but submitted the reports with Henry's name, and just as he had written them.

Common sense and tact achieved better results for Henry Small than any brash, vindictive, argumentative confrontations.

Office politics can be translated into diplomacy when "one puts one's foot down without stepping on anyone else's toes."

3. You and Your Secretary

"How To Get and Keep a Secretary" may soon become the executive's theme song. The secretarial supply is getting shorter than miniskirts, and, as the saying goes, any girl who gives a sign of breathing can get a job. She doesn't have to have any skills. Out of desperation, companies are beginning to offer on-the-job training, high pay, generous fringe benefits, liberal vacations, and Wall Street-type bonuses.

There was a time when a boss who allowed a secretary an extra hour for lunch to have her hair done was regarded as a paragon, a model of generosity and thoughtfulness with a profound understanding of female psychology. Now this sounds naive and picayune in comparison with the "beauty horoscope happening" one ad agency introduced for all its secretaries, complete with free cosmetics, new hair styling, and a reading of their astrological signs.

"Secretary's Day" used to be a happy, innocent affair, when department heads took their secretaries out for lunch. Office "in" jokes were in order, and every secretary was made to feel that her importance and contribution to the organization was appreciated.

But those were the good old days. Now the occasion has to be invested with excitement and hoopla, such as the Chicago company which provides each secretary with fifty dollars spending money for a Saturday at the racetrack.

Placement agencies, personnel directors, and recruiters are racing their mental motors, nursing ulcers, and biting their nails trying to find a way to snag employable secretaries, and then a formula to entice them to stay on the job.

One female management consultant, with a professional as well as a subjective understanding of women, has come up with what she feels is a solution. As yet she has not been successful in persuading one of her clients, a male-dominated mini-giant corporation, to take the plunge. It is the simple appeal to human frailty, irresistible vanity. The idea is to provide each secretary with attractive, designer-created "career costumes" to wear in the office, color coordinated, of course, to suit each girl. In addition, facilities are to be provided for weekly hair-styling and makeup sessions free of charge. The airlines have tried it, and there doesn't seem to be a shortage of stewardesses.

In the meantime, the secretarial gap is getting wider and wider, with disgruntled executives across the country yearning for the good old days when a secretary was a right arm, a discreet conscience, and an efficient helpmate.

"BE-KIND-TO-YOUR-SECRETARY" ERA

The boss who is lucky enough to have a devoted secretary makes sure to treat her with tender loving care. If he is not exactly courtly, he makes sure that he is exceedingly courteous, and even more important, thoughtful. He doesn't make changes in letters at 4:45 and expect her to retype them before she leaves; if she is a commuter, he doesn't burden her with last-minute instructions; and if she makes a mistake, he doesn't explode.

Whether you have your own private secretary, share one with your boss, or take what you can get from the secretarial pool, your attitude is the same: you are a professional career man using the company's resources to assist you in your workload.

A good secretary who is efficient, loyal, tactful, and discreet is the original answer to every boss's prayer. These qualities are encouraged if the boss remembers on occasion to tell her that she is efficient, and lets her know from time to time that he appreciates her loyalty, tact, and discretion.

DAY-TO-DAY COURTESIES

(1) A pleasant "good morning" to your secretary will start the day off right. When you leave in the evening, a "good night" out of the corner of your mouth, as you are dashing out the door, is "cut-rate" courtesy.

(2) Your secretary is human. She will appreciate small courtesies such as "thank you" and "please."

(3) Never reprimand or criticize your secretary in the presence of others.

(4) You may or may not call your secretary by her first name. How you address her and how she addresses you depend upon the company-wide posture determined by your top management and the tradition within.

(5) Even if your company is permissive about the use of first names, when you introduce your secretary to anyone, give her the courtesy of her full name. Don't demean her by inviting a stranger to regard her as part of the office furniture. The simple statement "My secretary, Miss Smith," or "Miss Margaret Smith," will suffice.

(6) You may have to ask her to do a personal errand for you during her lunch hour. The same privilege does not apply to your wife or children.

(7) If your secretary makes a mistake that triggers off an intramural trauma, don't let her hold the bag alone. She is your departmental responsibility. Anything that happens in your department is your direct concern, and you are accountable. A good administrator has to know how to troubleshoot with a minimum degree of friction and a maximum degree of courtesy.

(8) If your work load threatens an overtime session, try to alert your secretary in advance so that she can make suitable arrangements. She too has a private life, and the additional pay may not compensate her for the personal disruption.

(9) If it is emergency work and the hour is past midnight when you finish, help her in every way you can to find safe transportation. If she lives in an unsafe neighborhood, or in an out-of-the-way place, try to arrange for her to stay overnight in a hotel. It is not mandatory, but it would be the con-

siderate thing to do to see that she is accommodated in the
hotel before you depart for home.

THE SECRETARIAL PIPELINE

The company cafeteria is often a hidden reservoir of information beyond price. Between the tuna-fish sandwich and
the pie à la mode, the secretarial exchange of office gossip
would give the chairman of the board a more comprehensive,
penetrating view of the inner workings of his organization
than any carefully tailored report. Competitors don't go in
for cloak-and-dagger tactics, but if they did, the employees'
cafeteria would yield a bonanza.

Secretaries are in the position of knowing many things
about their departments and are frequently in possession of
facts that may not always come to light in the communications chasm. The secretaries are not necessarily violating confidences or revealing classified information. Many of them
maintain a closed-mouth policy and a boss-protective code.
But tidbits of news as to what's going on, new plans brewing,
or possible shifting of personnel may be dropped in the
course of conversation. The lower the echelon, the greater
the temptation to impress others with inside information.

An executive, whether he is top, middle, or lower, is only
human. Of course he will be receptive to any morsel of gossip his secretary may volunteer. The piece of news she brings
to him may be useful, and he is not likely to discourage the
practice. An executive may detest Machiavellian machinations, but he has to be in it because he has to be with it.
Business morality does not always operate under the accepted
rules of gentlemanly behavior. Intrigues and office politics exist in every corporation and at every level.

The secretarial pipeline works both ways. The inevitable
concern of how much she reveals about *your* business and
personal affairs has to be dealt with. Tact and courtesy are
the lines to pursue. Relate to her sense of loyalty, directing
the discussion within the framework of a team in which mutual trust and confidence should be respected. Cross-examin-
ing her is not advisable. She may interpret this as an infer-
ence that she has been indiscreet and that you find her un-
trustworthy. You will discourage her from bringing you any

more news, which is the last thing you want to do. Take her into your confidence and discuss the problem with her as though it were of mutual concern. Her intelligence and her sense of loyalty will react in your favor.

4. The Office Host

RECEIVING CALLERS IN YOUR OFFICE

Your private office is your home away from home. Visitors who come to your office are in effect your guests as well as the guests of your company. The professional image you project should be coated with the gracious, easy manners of a host.

The rules are simple, and like any social engagement, a few preparations in advance and proper manners with your visitor will make for smooth, unconfused preliminary dealings.

(1) When more than one visitor is expected, be sure there are enough comfortable chairs in your office before they arrive. Scrambling about for additional chairs while your guests stand and wait is time-consuming and disconcerting.

(2) Smoking has become one of those irksome problems that are producing a new crop of vocal disapprovers. Even if you are a nonsmoker, cigarettes and cigars as well as matches and clean ashtrays should be available for the guests who smoke.

(3) If you are a shirt-sleeve worker, it is polite to put on your jacket, whether your caller is a man or a woman. There are some diehard organizations, especially in the eastern metropolitan areas, where it is *de rigueur* for executives to wear jackets under all circumstances and under all conditions. Yet there are many evidences of a quiet revolution changing the old order in the sacrosanct chambers of business and govern-

ment. There is the story of a young executive aspirant who spent some time the night before brushing his suit and selecting a somber enough tie in order to appear before the president of a giant corporation, only to find him in shirt sleeves, an open collar, and a bright red waistcoat.

David Packard, former Deputy Secretary of Defense, is known to be a compulsive shirt-sleeve worker. While he was chairman and chief executive of the Hewlett-Packard Company, his employees knew that when his cuffs were near his wrists, all was serene, but the higher the shirt sleeves were rolled, the graver the problem.

In spite of the advent of air conditioning, more and more companies are tolerating jacketless executives. As with the use of first names, the rule of thumb is: large corporations are more formal than smaller companies. Geography also dictates the style an executive should pursue. In the Midwest, Southwest (Texas in particular), and on the West Coast, etiquette in general is more informal, and this is carried over into the business environment. Executives begin to discard their jackets when the temperature rises from hot to torrid. However, the unspoken rule is to wear a long-sleeved white shirt, with a tie neatly knotted. But, as Mark Twain said, "It's a good idea to obey all the rules when you are young, just so you'll have the strength to break them when you are old."

Recently a group of New York executives arrived in Phoenix in tightly buttoned business suits, complete with their attaché cases. Their Arizona counterparts, even the top-ranking executives, greeted them in their shirt sleeves. But what shirts! Beautifully tailored, obviously Savile Row-inspired, and with short sleeves.

A New York corporate division president, who maintains a first-name basis with his executives, nevertheless memoed them recently asking that jackets be worn in the office at all times.

Any young executive who has maverick compulsions will have to postpone them until such time as he is in a position to name the rules. For the time being he has to conform to top management's whims and fancies and, in any case, should always don the jacket when callers come.

(4) Circumstances beyond your control are the only valid excuse for keeping a guest, who has a definite appointment with you, cooling his impatience in the reception room until

you get ready to see him. If you know you will be late, the ideal thing, of course, is to notify him in advance and arrange the appointment for a later hour. If this is not possible, and if there is no way of avoiding the delay, make sure your caller is notified the moment he arrives that you will be late and that you extend your apologies, and hope he doesn't mind waiting for you. Wasting the time of any businessman is equivalent to robbing his wallet. Keeping him waiting is bad business practice and bad manners.

(5) If you cannot make your apologies in person, your secretary should explain the circumstances, and ask him if he would mind waiting. She might usher him into your private office, take his coat and hat, see that he is seated and is comfortable. She might ask him if he would like her to get him a magazine to read, or coffee or tea, or a soft drink while he is waiting for you.

This is routine in many organizations. In some of the larger corporations, especially in the new high-rise buildings, automatic vending machines are located on each floor with refreshments for employees as well as for visitors. Secretaries are known to keep a till of petty-cash coins to feed the machines. It is not unlikely that during a meeting in her boss's office a request will be made for refreshments, and an efficient secretary is prepared to oblige

(6) When the receptionist telephones you that your caller has arrived, the polite gesture is to have your secretary go to the reception room to escort the visitor to your office. If he is important and requires VIP treatment, you might go to the reception room yourself.

(7) Your secretary should be on hand in your office to accept the visitor's hat and coat, especially if there is more than one visitor. Many companies have special compartments to hang visitors' coats. A cluttered, untidy office is a distraction and not always conducive to relaxed discussions.

(8) When a visitor enters your office, you are the host and you naturally stand up. A firm handshake is a warm greeting of welcome, whether the caller is a male or a female. In Emily Post's day it was considered courteous for the man to wait for the woman to extend her hand first, but with the modern woman clamoring for equal rights, you will make her feel she belongs without offending her femininity by offering your hand first.

(9) One of the least endearing traits is to accept telephone

calls when you have visitors in your office, even if there is only one visitor and his rank is of no particular consequence. No person is comfortable sitting in your office professing indifference while you are carrying on a telephone conversation that is of no concern to him. Courtesy is an extension of one's character. Good breeding and consideration of others know no distinctions, and courtesy should, therefore, be a natural, unforced outgrowth of an innate sense of decency.

While you are in conference, your secretary, of course, will take messages. If a call comes through which in her judgment is important and requires your immediate attention, she might buzz you twice. Many executives work out signal systems with their secretaries, operating on President Nixon's theory that "a top-flight secretary has to have the skill of making hundreds of decisions for her employer, and she has to know what decisions not to make as well."

Before you answer the telephone, you might take a moment to apologize to your visitor, explaining that this call is important and that otherwise your secretary would not ring you.

(10) Your visitor may turn out to be a long-winded, nonstop talker. The pressures of many urgencies you still have to attend to are building up. Your nerves are taut and your temper is being severely tried. You can dispose of him with tact.

(a) If you have a prearranged signal system with your secretary, you might unobtrusively place your hand on your buzzer and ring her. If she enters with a questioning look, not too sure of what you want, you might resort to the signal John Daly, panel moderator of the TV program "What's My Line?" used. He would tug at his ear to communicate to the panel that their line of questioning was veering dangerously toward the risqué. If both your antennae are tuned in right, she will know and say, "I'm sorry to interrupt you, but you'll be late for your meeting," or words to that effect.

(b) A quicker and surer method is to stand up, telling your visitor how interesting and valuable you find your discussion and how much you wish you could continue it, but you are sorry, you have another appointment.

(11) When you rise to say good-bye, a warm handshake and a pleasant smile will send your visitor on his way with the best possible impression of you and, of course, of your

company. If he is a customer, or important to the company, you might escort him out of your office. Arthur Ochs Sulzberger, publisher of *The New York Times,* takes the time to show his visitors out as far as the anteroom. If your office is tucked away in a labyrinth of corridors, your secretary might lead your visitor as far as the reception room. This is much simpler and more polite than instructing him to turn right, then left, until he finds his way to the elevator.

The Unexpected Caller

Experienced executives or responsible businessmen seldom, if ever, drop in without an appointment. However, there are mitigating circumstances that are understandable. The visitor might have been on the premises meeting with one of the other executives of your company. He thought as long as he was there he might as well drop in on you just to say hello. He was motivated purely by friendship.

Good manners require that you greet him and exchange the usual pleasantries. If you are busy and under pressure, tell him so frankly. He is sure to understand and will not take up much of your time. A little politeness goes a long way and costs you nothing.

On the other hand, your unexpected caller may be your brother-in-law's cousin clutching a letter of introduction in his hot hand, requesting you to do all you can to help him. Or your visitor may be an old school chum who just breezed into town, and of course you're the first one he wants to see. In either event, you just have to grit your teeth and bear it. You may have to arrange a smile on your face, even give a warmish greeting, because it is precisely such minor crises that test the mettle of your executive poise and conduct.

TELEPHONE MANNERS

Telephonitis is an infectious disease, an affliction that is as common among men as it is among women. The cause is bad telephone manners—lack of consideration for the other person's time. For a convenience that is so important to modern living, and especially to industry, the telephone is too often converted into an instrument that is exasperating and a nuisance.

No organization, small or large, can afford to suffer from telephonitis. The Bell Telephone Company makes available members of their training staff to instruct switchboard operators, secretaries, and receptionists on how to use the telephone more efficiently and effectively. In addition, Bell maintains an extensive film library with professional commentators. Screenings are available to any company interested in "winning more friends by telephone," and to encourage their personnel to remember that "the voice with a smile" is as attractive as a smile on the face. These films are so lively and interesting that many management executives have been known to attend the screenings, together with the switchboard operators, secretaries, and receptionists.

The direct inward-dialing system allows executives to be reached at once without going through the time-consuming farce of talking to the switchboard operator, then being transferred to the secretary, who is obliged to go through the routine of asking, "May I tell Mr. Jones who is calling, please?" The caller may be unknown to the executive; he has to spell out his name to the secretary and perhaps even state his business, and more often than not the executive will have to talk to him anyway.

An amusing story used to make the rounds about a new secretary who did not take the trouble to pick up the phone when it rang. When her boss chided her about being derelict in her duty, she replied, "But all the calls are for you anyhow, so why should I bother?"

Most of the large companies are becoming increasingly attracted to the direct inward-dialing system because it is time-saving and makes good business sense. This system is usually a tie-line installation between the executive's and the secretary's desks, equipped with two or three digits and a buzzer device. This simplifies communication, especially if the executive has worked out a signal system with his secretary as to how he wants his calls treated.

In most cases, the trend is for the secretary to answer the telephone only when her boss is not available, is in conference, or for some reason wants his telephone calls screened. Some corporations still have to persuade their executives to answer their own telephones, but a good many executives are beginning to respond to the phone ring with the same reflex action as firemen do to the bell. When it rings they automatically answer.

There are no statistics available as yet on the number of companies or the type of corporation that prefers the direct inward-dialing system. A telephone official reports that from a cursory survey it was found that the old established firms, such as investment and banking houses, prefer secretaries to screen calls before transferring them to their superiors. This procedure applies primarily to the headquarters. Branch managers have begun to establish personal rapport with depositors by circulating not only their own direct dial numbers but also those of assistant managers in charge of mortgages and personal loans.

Good telephone manners are not only a reflection of courteous behavior; they are necessary to good business practice. Here are ten telephone commandments, elementary but important.

(1) Answer your telephone immediately. The persistent ringing of the phone is an annoyance to others in the surrounding offices and a waste of the caller's time.

(2) Identify yourself at once, saying, "Trevelyan Workhard speaking," or Trevelyan Workhard, Sales Department," adding your title if it is pertinent. Even Squaresville has dropped the "Hello."

Including the first name when introducing yourself over the telephone has had some curious responses in an age when conventional courtesies have fallen victim to shortcuts.

Stanley Fuller, who rose from salesman to sales manager and before the age of forty became president of a corporation, relates his experience: "I have always made it a policy when telephoning a customer, especially someone I did not know personally, to say, 'Is this Mr. Daniel Wyckoff? This is Stan Fuller of Consolidated.' This was an open invitation to him to call me by my first name. Establishing instant friendly contact with a customer is a proven sales approach which, for me anyway, has been profitable. If the customer was not immediately responsive, but called me 'Mr.,' naturally I called *him* 'Mr.' in return. If he showed an interest in me and my products, by the end of the conversation I would suggest, 'Call me Stan, why don't you?' And his response invariably would be 'Sure. And my name's Dan.'"

(3) The telephone call might have interrupted something you were doing or thinking about. Don't let your voice be-

tray your irritation. Switch on your friendly, cheerful tone, which is a sure guarantee to start off the conversation on a pleasant note. If your caller happens to be an irate customer, or someone with a complaint, a friendly, warm receptiveness on your part is likely to disarm him.

(4) It is polite to wait for the caller to say good-bye, unless you are terribly pressured, in which case you'll have to find an appropriate excuse to bring the call to a not too brusque finish. If you are not too hasty, the call may turn out to be profitable in last-minute orders or meaningful information.

(5) Hang up gently. A receiver slammed in the ear of the caller is like slamming the door after a visitor. It may not be intentional, but the effect is the same.

(6) If your secretary answers the telephone, the most business-like procedure is for her to say, "Good morning. Mr. Workhard's office." Or "Mr. Workhard's secretary, Miss Jones, speaking."

(7) If you are not available to take the call, your secretary should explain politely that she is sorry but you are in conference, or that you are not in your office, but that perhaps she can be of help. It is quite possible that she will be. An efficient secretary can be relied upon to find out the purpose of the call, and if she cannot supply the information herself, she can prepare her boss so that when he returns the call he will have all the facts before him.

(8) If your secretary telephones someone for you, she should buzz you as soon as she hears him give his name (or however he acknowledges the call). You, the executive, should answer immediately. Nothing is more exasperating or impolite to a person than to be called and then to be expected to hang on to a mute telephone until you get around to picking up your phone.

(9) When you telephone someone yourself, and his secretary answers, if she does not know you, you may wish to give her a quick rundown as to who you are and the reason for your call. This is a time-saver for both of you, as well as for the person whom you are calling.

(10) When a secretary telephones and tells your secretary that Mr. Stranger wishes to speak to Mr. Hardwork, your secretary might ask, "Is Mr. Stranger ready to come to the phone, because I can put Mr. Hardwork on immediately."

Even if you are not seen when speaking on the telephone,

you are nevertheless on parade. A pleasant voice, a clear mind, and an outgoing personality always come through. Speak briefly and to the point, and even if the call is a disagreeable one, follow the proverb that "a soft answer turneth away wrath."

5. Business Meetings

THE CORPORATE WAY OF LIFE

Some companies discourage a plethora of meetings, operating on the theory that too many executives already spend too much of their time at bull sessions, often talking about the very things they should be doing. Nevertheless, meetings are on the increase, partly because of mergers and acquisitions, which call for the realignment of executive responsibility, policy changes, production goals, and long-term planning. One divisional manager, whose company was the victim of a take-over by a larger corporation, estimates that in a thirty-day period, he spent no more than nine hours at his desk. The rest of the time was taken up with various meetings and discussions. Top-of-the-head thinking is no longer enough. The combined brainpower, experience, and skills of responsible executives are required.

Essentially, a business meeting is a "think session," a meeting of minds in which each representative has a contribution to make, whether as an active participant or as an observer.

The company conference room is the mirror that exposes you before your toughest and perhaps most critical audience—your superior officers, your colleagues, and your subordinates. Every nuance of expression, mannerism, and speech reveals who you are and what you can do. The conference room is the nerve center of the company, where your behavior and your manners will indicate to your superiors on which rung of the ladder you belong.

As a young executive scheduled to attend a company meeting, it would be the better part of judgment to tidy your mind and your nerves with the same meticulous attention that you give to your personal appearance. Blueprint your behavior pattern in advance very much as you would prepare an agenda.

The tidying process should begin with banishing from your mind all the negatives. Young executives are prone to regard entering the conference room as somewhat like walking into the executive jungle, where everyone present is a potential tiger.

Walk into the room with an easy, relaxed stride, demonstrating that you are in full command of yourself. Check your wisecracks and flippancies. Leave them in the bottom drawer of your desk. Even if the meeting proves to be cliché-ridden, dull, and plodding, think only of the plus angle: business meetings produce the adrenalin that sustains the corporate body.

If you are a young executive, you can learn how to play your company by the simple expedient of following the leaders. Some corporations are more formal than others. Take your cue from the older executives in terms of tenure or age. They have accepted the rules, or they may have set them up.

Your conduct, your attention span, your personality, your participation, and especially your involvement will be the facets by which your superiors will judge your total leadership potential.

Let us assume that you are either a middle-management executive, one with administrative and supervisory authority to carry out company policies and introduce company objectives, or a junior executive, possibly a graduate from one of the major business administration schools, with two to eight years' experience. In both cases there are three basic types of meetings in which you will be expected to play a part.

(1) The meeting in which you are in observer representing your superior or your divisional group.

(2) The meeting in which you are a participant.

(3) The meeting for which you are responsible and which you might have to conduct.

THE MEETING IN WHICH
YOU ARE AN OBSERVER

Your Role

Your role is essentially that of a reporter and not that of an opinion maker. Your efforts will be directed toward getting as much clear-cut information as possible without any inconsequential intrusions on your part.

Since you are there primarily as a listener, you are not expected or required to speak.

Here are some simple do's and don'ts to remember:

(1) Come to the meeting promptly, even a little early.

(2) On entering or leaving the conference room the young executive, without making too much of a show, would do well to step aside to allow the company officials, high-level executives, or older managers to go first.

(3) In some companies formalities are adhered to: younger men rise when the top brass enter the room and wait until they take their seats. Other companies are less formal. Again, the clues should be taken from the older participants.

(4) Obvious signs of inattention, shuffling of papers, glancing out of the window, whispering with your neighbor, or any signs of fidgeting are all irritants that are sure to redound against you.

(5) If one of the speakers turns out to be a crashing bore, arrange your expression to appear interested and involved.

(6) The pad and pencil on the table in front of your chair were not placed there for doodling. It is an implied offense to the speaker as well as to the chairman. Notetaking not only demonstrates that you are on the alert, but it also flatters the speaker.

(7) If your neighbor whispers to you during the meeting, answer him with a smile or a wink or some facial expression to indicate that you got the message and that you will communicate with him later.

Should You Ask Questions?

You may ask questions, but only on such points as require clarification. It is not advisable to inject new directions or alternatives unless you have received specific instructions from your superior to do so.

Think your questions through carefully, and if you feel they have any validity, present them. Be relevant and concise. Popping up with too many questions or projecting half-baked ideas just for the sake of underscoring your presence may prove an irritant to the elder statesmen, and, in fact, everyone present.

Young executives who have been professionally schooled and who have up-to-the-minute knowledge of the latest developments in automation, data processing, and the new mathematics may have an advantage over some of their yesterday-minded top brass. Not only good manners but good common sense should warn the tomorrow-minded executive to beware of the loaded question, or any question that might prove an embarrassment to others, especially to any of the participants at the meeting.

In fact, a casual complimentary reference to a previous speaker will be a score in your favor. But be careful you do not sound patronizing. This is an inexcusable blunder of bad taste.

Reporting the Results to Your Superior

The minutes of any meeting of consequence are generally recorded by the appointed or elected secretary of the group, or by a stenographer, stenotypist, or tape recorder. But your superior officer may wish to get a firsthand report from you, the junior executive who is representing him at the meeting.

Your boss can read the hard cold facts in the minutes. What he expects from you is the meat that fills out the skeleton, the overtones that brought certain conclusions to a head, the organizational posture assumed by top management, as well as your own evaluation of the meeting and perhaps your reactions to its conclusions.

A group of young executives might get together in the back room and joke about the meeting; that "it started at 9:30 A.M. sharp and ended at 11:45 dull." But when you are reporting to the head of your department, it may be wise for you to refrain from frivolous or extraneous remarks. How you communicate with your boss depends, of course, upon the rapport that exists between you. But even if the camaraderie between you and your superior is on a first-name basis, and even if you have dined in each other's homes and your wives liked each other, in the office you must still walk the tightrope, that subtle demarcation of the subordinate vis-à-vis his boss. In the general scheme, it is best to give an objective, straightforward evaluation of the meeting.

During the discussions with your superior his own biases are likely to reveal themselves. He might interject denigrating remarks about the meeting and especially about some of his colleagues. Sidestep these as tactfully as you can without falling into his trap.

Reporting the Results to Your Departmental or Divisional Group

Should your report be written or oral? There are no rigid rules for this type of meeting. In the main such sessions are informal, and your report may be presented orally.

As the principal speaker you are in the spotlight. You will be rated by management as well as your peers on your performance and presentation, your effectiveness, your leadership potential, and especially on your grasp of the issues involved.

THE MEETING IN WHICH YOU ARE A PARTICIPANT

Departmental or Sectional Meetings

The average young executive is most likely to participate in group sessions relating to his departmental or sectional responsibilities and programs. These get-togethers are work sessions, the discussions being slanted toward routine issues, fact-finding, problem-solving, brainstorming, or planning a course of action. The meetings are usually informal, attended by persons with whom the young executive works or deals on frequent occasions. Each person at the meeting is involved in the total work force, on which the ultimate effectiveness of his department is dependent.

The young executive must bear in mind that good participation at a meeting does not begin or end in the conference

room. Preliminary analysis, strategy format, guidelines—
these are all helpful preparatory steps.

A brain-picking session with his immediate superior is essential. It is implicit that the boss's viewpoint be upheld and
not bucked at an open meeting. Any proposals or recommendations the junior executive wishes to make should be discussed with his immediate superior before presentation at the
meeting.

An assessment of the foreseeable attitudes of the other
participants might be analyzed to avoid, if possible, the risks
of misunderstandings and conflicts.

The Company-Wide and Interdepartmental Meetings

Company-wide meetings are usually formal. Most often they
have one or more speakers, each of whom represents a specialized facet of the meeting. Few young or new executives
are invited to participate on such occasions, the speaker's
platform being relegated to the more seasoned executives.
But if you have the fortune to be invited to speak, bear in
mind that it is not only you but your superior and, in fact,
your whole department that are on view. This is the rare
chance when you can show top executive promise by voice,
by words, by manner, and by manners. This is your chance
to attract management's interest, while you present your department's viewpoint.

The interdepartmental meetings are less formal than the
company-wide meetings. This is because they are target-cen-
tered and serve special functions, such as, for example, the
interchange of ideas, coordination between departments and
sections, scheduling, expediting, and so on. The meetings may
represent only two departments, but they may also include a
great many units of the company.

Active participation is the name of the game. Each department is expected to make its contribution if the meeting is to
accomplish its goal.

Such meetings are of inestimable value to the middle-management executive; they underscore his executive talent and
his role as a "company man." For the junior executive they
are a continuing seminar on techniques in business management. The conditioning and insights gained by alert listening,
watching, and participating will pave the road toward future

leadership. Today's participant may be tomorrow's chairman of the meeting, hopefully escalating to higher and higher echelon recognition.

THE MEETING THAT YOU CONDUCT

Your Meeting

Some companies thrust their young executives into the responsibility of running a meeting as a sort of "trial by bloodbath," a way of proving whether they have executive leadership. Such a meeting is a showcase for the young executive to demonstrate that he knows how to plan, conduct, and "human-engineer" a meeting with the most productive results.

Most probably he would be assigned to conduct one of the regular periodic meetings, in which case an important part of his premeeting preparation should be a conference with his superior, whose policies and ideas must be upheld and implemented.

As a rule of thumb, a junior or middle-management executive should not presume to call a meeting unless he is confident that such a meeting is necessary. There may be occasions when a crisis situation arises which requires the combined thinking of the departmental personnel. His superior may be out of town or otherwise unavailable. If he does have to call a gathering of the "clan," the executive must be guided by what he knows to be his superior's policy. He must also use his judgment about his method of procedure and whether the company as such is meeting-minded.

Planning the Meeting

Careful premeeting planning and programming are a *must*. The blueprint should be clear and precise as to the issues to be discussed and the goals to be achieved. This applies to regular and periodic meetings, but even more so to ad hoc sessions and calls for emergency get-togethers.

(1) Notification. Notices for regular meetings are routine. In some companies the time schedule is prearranged. Certain days of the month are set aside for periodic meetings. For special or ad hoc meetings, advance notice of two to five

days is a good margin. Shorter notice might indicate an emergency; if such is the case, it should be so stated. The two-to-five-day timing is a safe bet, giving the expected participants time to adjust their calenders and to assure a good attendance. An executive who earns a reputation for running a meeting in a business-like fashion, with the ability to pace the discussions toward a maximum of fertile decisions within a limited time period, will be sure to get a good response to a meeting which he is scheduled to conduct.

(2) Participants. Only those persons who are directly concerned with the subject to be discussed or those who can be expected to make valid contributions should be asked to the meeting. Overstaffing a meeting opens it up to a possible free-for-all with too many diverse opinions. Moreover, it is a waste of the company's manpower and a needless expenditure of valuable working time to expect fringe executives to participate. Ordinarily, one representative from each department should suffice. To ensure a controlled, functional exchange of ideas, the attendance should be limited to about fifteen. A larger group may prove unwieldy for a young executive who is just beginning to flex his leadership muscles.

(3) The agenda. There should be no ifs or buts about sending the agenda in advance. It should accompany the memo announcing the meeting. The agenda will state clearly the subjects that are under consideration. A chairman who wishes to run an effective meeting leaves nothing to chance. Alerting the participants about the issues to be discussed and the goals (hopefully) to be achieved gives each attending member a chance to clarify his point of view. Also, he may wish to bring with him factual material pertaining to the problems at hand.

(4) Attendance. When routing the memo announcing the meeting, which will have the agenda attached, list all the names of the persons who are expected to attend. It will help each conferee to anticipate the different points of view and possible oppositions to the position he expects to maintain. List the names alphabetically so that there will be no repercussions about rank or position, and no bruised egos.

Stage-Managing the Meeting

(1) The Meeting Room. Make sure the conference room that is selected is large enough to accommodate the partici-

pants comfortably. There should be a sufficient number of chairs without crowding. The capacity of the mind to absorb is limited to what the seat can endure. Physical discomfort can charge the air with tension.

The chair at the head of the table is for the chairman. There is no need to assign seats at informal meetings. In many cases, the younger executives would be wise to wait for departmental heads or older participants to occupy the chairs flanking the leader; the younger men can fall in farther down the line.

Pads and pencils should be placed on the table before each seat. Don't forget a few ashtrays for smokers. A thoughtful gesture would be to have a pitcher of fresh water and drinking glasses placed on a convenient side table.

(2) Tape-recording the Meeting. Some persons think that if a meeting is not important enough to warrant recording the proceedings, it may not be important enough to be held. Psychological studies in memory retention reveal that attendees remember only those issues that suit their own best interests.

A tape recorder is a simple solution. It not only will keep the record straight for the leader but will be a word-for-word report of what transpired. There can be no arguments or disavowals at a later date as to the decisions reached, particularly those decisions requiring recommendations for a future course to follow.

However, there are occasions when a tape recorder in full view might impede free discussion and a frank exchange of opinions. In that case, the chairman will have to rely on his memory, or have a secretary take notes as the discussion proceeds.

(3) Visual Aids. You may find that you will save time and get your points across if you add visual aids to your meeting. Office planners recognize the vital role visual aids play in large or small meeting rooms. Most are now equipped with blackboards, roll-up maps, screens, and other necessary paraphernalia.

According to a study made some years ago at the Ordnance School, Aberdeen Proving Grounds, Maryland, "People of all ages and mental capacities are more attentive when they see the point illustrated as well as hear it; they understand it quicker—remember it longer." The study indicated that we *retain* approximately:

10% of what we read
20% of what we hear
30% of what we see
50% of what we see and hear

For a meeting to achieve maximum effectiveness, a chairman might plan his presentation to appeal to the eye as well as to the mind. Your listeners may learn from what you say, but they will retain much more if they see the ideas, facts and figures graphically illustrated.

An enterprising young executive should have no problem obtaining suitable visual aids. If he is clued in, he'll make the most of the creative resources within the corporate setup— the advertising, publicity, and research departments. They are sure to have, or can produce, professional charts, photographs, and diagrams to spark the meeting. The advertising department, especially, working in the graphic arts media, should be able to come up with something dramatic and impressive.

(4) Scenario. An interesting meeting is a successful meeting. It need not adhere strictly to the code of banality. It should be stage-managed just as any play or movie if it is to capture and hold the interest of the audience. In addition to the agenda, a wise and forward-thinking chairman will prepare a scenario *pacing* his meeting so that all salient features are covered, and no yawning loopholes are possible. He will also have to find ways and means to soft-pedal controversial topics, which he must anticipate and be ready to cope with.

His script should include at least three elements.

(a) His opening remarks should be brief and to the point. His function is to *present* the problem; the meeting's function is to discuss the problem and come to some conclusions and suggested solutions. A long-winded opening takes the edge off the urgency of the meeting and leaves the participants "dumb at one end and numb at the other."

(b) A few amusing anecdotes and perhaps a joke or two will help to clear the air if tensions build up. Nothing risqué, of course, or blood pressures may rise to the indignation level.

(c) A chairman would be wise to take a premeeting census of his conferees, and prepare himself with leading questions. The most important are questions that will spotlight the points specified on the agenda, in case the issues get side-tracked in the heat of discussion. A perceptive analysis of each personality, as well as some individual idiosyncrasies, may suggest the right questions to ask to help play the ego game.

The Chairman's Function in Keeping Order

(1) A gavel is undesirable. The meeting participants may assume that your private IBM machine has punched you up a notch or two above your level. The gentle tapping of a pencil on a glass, or projecting your voice slightly above the hubbub, will do the trick. *Robert's Rules of Order* states that "standing very quietly may accomplish surprising results."

(2) Keep calm even when the going is rough. Don't lose your temper, however justified or soul-satisfying that may be. A chairman's role is a dual one: that of the leader of the meeting and that of an arbitrator. If the chairman loses his objectivity and impartiality, he loses control of the meeting. He cannot and should not take sides in any debate, and he should at all costs avoid personality conflicts.

(3) Private conversations should be discouraged with tact and courtesy. Catching the eye of the talker sometimes works. If not, the chairman might say to the person who has the floor: "Just a minute, please." Then turning to the offender say: "Dan, you may have the floor just as soon as Frank finishes what he has to say." One chairman broke up a private conversation with a subtle gambit. He addressed himself to the man who was the captive audience of a persistent talker by saying: "Richard, stop listening, please."

(4) The meeting monopolizer should be controlled, but handled politely so that he is not offended. Interrupt him at the end of a sentence by telling him he is making a great contribution to the meeting, but that there are a few others who still have to be heard from. You might add that if there is time you'll call on him again.

(5) Meetings with an assemblage of competing personalities are sometimes breeding grounds for arguments. A chairman must be on the alert to guard against such contingencies. A minor argument starting on a low key can explode into high-voltage intensity. An experienced conference leader found a simple solution. If a heated argument broke out between two members, he would walk to the trouble spot, place

his hands gently on the shoulders of the vociferous arguers, and at the same time ask a pointed question of someone across the room. This is a diplomatic and courteous way of stopping the argument and directing the meeting back to its purpose.

(6) The perennial debater. Every large organization is plagued with a know-it-all. His position is "You're wrong and I'm right." A chairman would be wise to follow Robert Frost's dictum that one has to listen to almost anything without losing one's temper or one's self-confidence. The chairman, alas, must allow the compulsive debater to have his say—within reason. Then, he can venture to interrupt him by saying something like: "You are making some valid points, but we haven't heard from Harry Parker yet, and we ought to get his opinion on the subject."

(7) The inarticulate or silent type. It is expected that every attendee has a contribution to make; otherwise he would not have been invited to the meeting. It is up to the chairman to draw on the thinking of *all* the members. If he has prepared himself with a sufficient number of pertinent questions to ask, he will have a potent, direct query to encourage the silent one to speak up and make his departmental contribution for the enlightenment of the meeting as a whole.

At the End of the Meeting

(1) Summing Up. This is when the chairman's leadership is put to the test. His summing up at the conclusion of the meeting is the barometer that will indicate whether the investment of time and energy has paid off.

The chairman should briefly outline the decisions reached, clarifying the points of differences and stating clearly the future steps to be taken.

A few well-chosen words of appreciation thanking the participants for their contributions are in order.

(2) Follow-Up. A short written summary reporting the decisions reached at the meeting, underlining the necessary actions to be taken and sent to all the participants, is a safeguard well worth the time and effort.

Again a word of thanks is a salutary gesture that is sure to be appreciated.

RULES FOR ALL MEETINGS

Preliminaries

Do your homework before entering the conference room. In most corporations it is a matter of policy to distribute in advance either the agenda or a memo outlining the salient points to be discussed. If no such information is forthcoming, the secretarial grapevine, employed with tact and without attempting to violate any confidences, can be helpful.

Study the issues involved, and if necessary research the background. Knowledge breeds confidence.

Protocol

Parliamentary procedure represents the courtesies that smooth the progress of more formal meetings. The cardinal rules are basically those inherent in good social conduct.

(1) Punctuality is a self-evident factor. If possible, come a little earlier. One of the secrets of successful participation at a meeting is the rapport you achieve with the other individuals. Try for a "reading" of the climate, chatting with other participants who have come ahead of time, probably for the same reason you have.

(2) Speak only when the chairman gives you the nod. Once you are on your feet, do not hog the floor. Even if the subject under discussion is your specialty, do not indulge yourself in too much self-projection. An ambitious young executive, secure in his knowledge, should rein in his self-importance and pace his presentation to the tempo of the meeting. Older executives who have not had the same advantages of professional schooling may take a dim view of any arrogant display of knowledge. Above all, remember: *Every word you say is being recorded in the minutes.*

(3) Do not interrupt another speaker with whose point of view you disagree. A small disagreement can develop into a large controversy. Wait until he has finished, then ask for the floor. If you are in the lower echelon, it might be wiser for you not to air your difference at the meeting. You may be sure of your facts, but you will not endear yourself to the

older executives if you overplay your hand. An after-the-meeting face-to-face discussion might iron out the bothersome points and win you an ally.

(4) When other speakers disagree with you, maintain an objective attitude. Do not personalize your counterattack. Respect the rights of others to disagree with you, even though you are convinced you are right. Listen to what they have to say, then offer your rebuttal when the chairman gives you the floor.

(5) Give credit where credit is due. If a speaker has projected an idea you can go along with, indicate your agreement. This is not toadying favor but is good human relations.

(6) Humor at a meeting is a double-edged sword. The lower the echelon, the greater the need to temper the jokes, wisecracks, and the most horrendous of sins, sarcasm. If the chairman is inclined to be jocular, join in the laughter. Show your appreciation for someone else's witticisms. If you cannot stop yourself from producing your own favorite *bon mot*, make sure it does not discredit or humiliate anyone present. A young man with a promising future in an insurance company lost his job because, when some statistics presented by a senior VP were being discussed, he quipped: "However you figure it, it's like a beautiful woman without any legs to stand on."

(7) Do not surprise your boss with a proposal he knows nothing about. If you have not previously talked over the subject with him, cool it until you get a chance to do so. If your boss agrees that the proposal has merit, he will agree to have the idea routed to the various departments or proposed at the next meeting.

(8) At the end of the meeting, do not be among the first to leave the conference room. Stand up and enter into casual conversation with some of the other participants. This will permit the high-level executives to make their exits first. You will show proper deference without making a to-do about it.

The Post-Factum Syndrome

Corporate meetings of all types, large or small, are a valuable testing ground for executive material. Each participant, whether he is aware of it or not, is being evaluated. Job security haunts the middle-aged as well as the young executives. Post-meeting jitters are occupational hazards.

"How did I make out?" may not be articulated, but it haunts the conscience.

Did you win the admiration of your fellow participants, and more important, did you invite their goodwill? Winning their admiration does not necessarily imply that they like you. They may admire you for what you know but at the same time thoroughly dislike you.

You must channel your energies to win the respect, approval, and liking of your fellow workers. Once they like you as a person, a human being practicing the basic tenets of decency and courtesy, admiration for your working abilities will naturally follow. Moreover, gaining their goodwill and their approval will be tantamount to oiling the wheels in order to get you to your objective faster and with greater ease.

A good example is the exceptionally gifted young executive in an investment counseling firm who came to see me. He had everything going for him. A cum laude graduate from an Ivy League college, he was charming, personable, dressed in good taste, and his manners were impeccable. His initial relationship with his colleagues left nothing to be desired. They lunched together, exchanged personal views, and related family anecdotes.

His immediate superior had so much faith in this promising young man that he was grooming him for advancement in the company, which was a fast-growing one.

But soon the young man became enamored with the "bright boy" image of himself and became obsessed with living up to that image at all times. He invariably tried to impress everyone and on all occasions. When knotty problems were discussed at meetings, his agile mind produced feasible recommendations before anyone else had a chance to do so.

At first his superiors were impressed. They would stop to chat with him after the meeting; they would ask him how he had arrived at such-and-such conclusion; and they showed every indication that his agile and insightful mind was duly appreciated. But after a time, they and his colleagues became restive. The young man began to sense a coolness. Once or twice at meetings somebody would say: "Why not ask Bob? He always seems to have all the answers."

He became increasingly alarmed when others received promotions and he continued to remain behind. He confronted his superior and demanded to know the reason. He was told frankly: "You've got a problem, Bob, and if I were you, I'd go for help. You measure up in every area but one. You are too much of a know-it-all. You're not liked for that reason. The other men have found out how smart you are, but they hate your guts."

His self-confidence was undermined; his usefulness to the company diminished; and eventually he was asked to leave.

This is an example of wasting too much energy to impress. Bob had reversed the basic principle of good working relationships. His efforts should have been directed to being liked and being accepted.

CONVENTIONS

If you are thinking of conventions as the "old-time meeting of the bored," forget it. There is much entertainment and razzle-dazzle, and the essential message comes through, sometimes in psychedelic colors, sometimes in neon lights, sometimes in Pop art. No delegate leaves without a bulging baggage of information and inspiration, unless he is a dunderhead.

A good example is a soft-drink company's two-day session for its bottlers, which all agreed was a "bubbling good show." As reported in *Meetings & Conventions:* "To simulate a feeling of complete involvement and encourage a full sense of two-way communication, a uniquely new stage, screen, and projection design and construction" were introduced. "Unusual screen shapes added a three-dimensional effect to the projected slides which numbered over 1,500.... In addition, stretched fabric sails on the sides of the room were used as projection surfaces to punctuate important segments of the total meeting message. They were also employed to jar and stimulate the audience during transitions, bridges, and introductions. At various times psychedelic lights, strobes, color wheels, and multiple slide images heightened and held audience interest."

Both live and taped talent were used liberally throughout the meeting, with a spectacular presentation of the new advertising campaign for all product lines, introduced through audio-visual slide and film spectaculars. Other highlights included individual presentations on the coming plans for each of the company's products.

Meetings & Conventions further reports that the audience "response was enthusiastic throughout the presentation" and that the "meeting indicated that the conference had met all its communication goals and served as a highly successful launch pad for the coming year."

It is difficult to ascertain the amount of money spent on conventions. The International Association of Conventions estimates that between 2.5 and 3 billion dollars are spent each year. But this does not include "less than convention" get-togethers, where new products, sales promotion, and other program planning take place. Some qualified experts place that figure at 5 to 7 billion, which brings the total to between 7.5 and 10 billion dollars annually.

For a young executive the convention scene is a proving ground where he is frequently assigned to an active role, but, even without a definite assignment, he cannot afford to remain passive.

6. Communication: Word of Mouth

"Communicating" has entered the word game; if you are not with it, you are not in it. Communicating is not only understanding others, but making others understand you. The media cover every aspect of human interchange from speech to the written word to the face you present while listening, observing, thinking. Your mien, your actions, your expression, and your general stance will tell as much about you as the words you utter. Your ultimate goal is to inspire confidence in the man you are.

It is not possible for a man to absorb everything that comes across his desk or over the telephone. In self-defense, he has become a scanner and a skimmer in his reading and a half-listener in his hearing.

Corporations spend huge sums of money to introduce better communication *systems*, but until they can invent the mechanical man who can think clearly, speak with authority, and write business letters and reports that win friends and customers, it rests upon the human individual to perform these tasks according to his personal style.

Emerson said that "speech is power. Speech is to persuade, to convert, to compel." But there is also a time to know when and how to listen, and to relate to the person with whom you are communicating.

"One of the hardest things in the world," Lewis Carroll wrote in *Alice in Wonderland*, "is to convey meaning accurately from one mind to another." And when Alice said: "Really, now you ask me, I don't think—," the Mad Hatter warned her: "Then you shouldn't talk."

DO WE SPEAK THE SAME LANGUAGE?

Generation after generation has enriched the American language with its own idioms, often lively and refreshing, and just as often, as in today's culture, with a sock-it-to-'em quality.

The new lingo has been taken up by the "squares"—sometimes referred to as the "octagons," who are the supersquares, or the "rubes," who are just average squares. All squares are "telling it like it is," though ironically, the new phrases they are "mouthing" stem from the out groups—the alienated, the activists, and the discontented. Literary critic Philip Rahv laments that " 'tell it like it is' is the supreme cliché of the year."

Hippiedom's jargon is colorful and often potent. Radio and TV air waves are spiced with such phrases as "freaked out" and "soul power," and commentators are showing increasing inclination to "dig the scene," like any miniskirted teeny-bopper. The same applies to newspaper columnists and journalists, who are echoing the underground press, which is spewing out newspapers, magazines, and books from the East Village to Haight-Ashbury.

The language barrier places many a young executive in a dangling position between a Marshall McLuhan spaceout and the business world to which he is committed: a dilemma which leaves him little choice if he has the bad habit of enjoying three meals a day and a decent roof over his head.

At an informal brainstorming session held in the headquarters of one of the giant automobile companies, a young executive was holding forth. He was directing his remarks to an associate who had just presented a workable idea. "It's not quite my bag," he said, "but if you want me to tune in on it with you, just give me a nudge."

With a half smile, the manager of his division asked, "Is that hippie talk, Bob? I know what you're trying to say, but we're all kind of square around here, you know ..." Quickwittedly, the young man interposed, "But Mr. Stricker, it's the squares who've made the world go round." And that saved the day for Bob.

Another curious incident occurred when an executive

referred to someone as a "fink." It was his secretary who called him to task, telling him, "That word doesn't sound quite right coming from you." Which calls to mind *New York Times* columnist Russell Baker's statement that "people used to want to grow up. Now they just want to sound young."

Whether any of the hippie-Yippie-inspired words and phrases will survive long enough to be included in the next edition of the unabridged dictionary is hard to foretell. Fashions in dialogue are unpredictable and ever changing, but the Establishment, represented by business and industry, adheres to the formalities and sternly rejects newfangled quirks in any shape or form.

There is a contradiction in the Establishment's attitude. The mainstream of business and industry is space-age action, but the expected behavior patterns are strictly Emily Post. Corporations spend millions of dollars to explore and develop the most modern, the most far-out technological-electronic-computerized systems; they think nothing of discarding old, outdated equipment and introducing new ones at great expense. But when it comes to human conduct, human appearance, speech, and behavior, the guidelines are clearly defined by etiquette's timeworn standards and formalities.

A young executive who values his career and his reputation in the business world should encounter no hardships if he employs the King's English in his speech as well as in his written words. Fashions in jargon and idiom change as frequently as fashions in clothes. Words are the coins that make up the currency of sentences. The use of the right, the pertinent, words adds up to meaningful dollars and sense.

Communication is useless unless what is said or written is understood. An executive who has to instruct or direct subordinates has an obligation to make himself understood. And he can do so only by speaking plainly, simply, and without reference to fad phrases, local dialects, or technical terms that will cause his listeners or his readers to furrow their brows and make them wonder what it is all about. The only sure way of communicating is simply—using the layman's language in two-syllable words which say what you have to say and which are understood by the persons you are addressing face-to-face, on the telephone, in a letter, or from a public platform.

YOU AND PUBLIC SPEAKING

The message is the media, and at the rate that organizational communications are expanding, the average executive will have to polish his speaking style. His daily schedule may program him for personal appearances anywhere from a departmental confab in a small meeting room to a panel in a sales-marketing conference or as a spokesman on a mass-media platform, either in an auditorium or through the channels of TV or radio.

Progressive management-thinking is creating its own juggernaut for mass communication. In addition to routine intraorganizational meetings, today's executives are involved in an ever-broadening circle of speaking engagements due to several factors:

(1) The invasion of closed-circuit television into the corporate way of life.

(2) The advent of Picturephone, the "see-you-as-you-talk" telephone system.

(3) With the mushrooming of conglomerates, the ever growing numbers of conventions, where no executive is an invisible man, he is often required to take an active part in a private caucus and, at all times, he functions as an official host to visiting delegates, customers, and distributors.

(4) Industry's accelerated concern with public affairs is placing an onus upon executives as spokesmen before civic and community groups.

(5) Increased demands on articulate executives to appear as panelists or speakers in auditoriums, on radio and television.

No matter on which platform or in which capacity an executive is scheduled to speak, he is giving a sales talk. He is selling himself as well as his company. His personality, his voice, his appearance, become part and parcel of his message—a packaged presentation designed to make a lasting impression upon his audience.

Executives have been known to take elocution lessons to rid themselves of regional and provincial speech foibles. Now they may be required to take courses in The Living Theatre or even explore the possibilities of The Method.

Before an executive panics or gives in to a threatening sense of inadequacy, here is a crash program he might follow if he wants to look and sound right. These are security measures whether he is appearing at a meeting with his superiors, peers, or subordinates, whether on a platform before a large audience, before a microphone, on closed or open television, or is dialed in on Picturephone.

Relax!

True, easier said than done. But you can always fall apart later. It helps to remember that you are not unique and that you are not really an oddball. Even the most seasoned actors and public speakers admit to being nervous and tense before making an appearance.

Practice in Front of Your Mirror

Stand in front of a full-length mirror and confront yourself as though you were an important audience. Talk aloud, giving yourself a good speech, telling yourself there is nothing to fear but fear itself. This is one way of banishing your fears. The mirror may also reveal to you mannerisms which you may not be aware of and which you may wish to correct.

(1) Facial expressions should not be overdone. A beginner is likely to try to ham it, when all he has to do is be himself. Just remember—you are speaking person-to-person. Excessive grimacing and eye blinking will tell your audience what you least want them to know—that you are nervous. You want your audience to laugh *with* you and not *at* you, so give them an occasional smile or a wide grin.

(2) Gestures and movements help to create interest. If you are inclined to make gestures to illustrate a point, by all means do so. Hand language is a thesaurus in itself. Mother's repeated warning, "Don't point," has lost its meaning. If you want to single out an object or make a decisive statement, your index finger will do it for you effectively. If you are one of those who like to emphasize each point by counting them off on your fingers, it may strengthen your verbal comments. In other words, do what comes naturally to you. But here again, don't overdo the gestures. Contrived or artificial movements may be laugh-provoking, turning you into a caricature of yourself. So are continuous nervous motions, such as

"shooting" your shirt cuffs or continually fussing with your pocket handkerchief. For a stand-up talk, you may be tempted to place your hands in your pockets. This is not always a happy solution. You are likely to jingle your coins or keys, which may be irritating to your listeners. Watching yourself in your mirror you will see yourself as others will see you, and you will know when to make gestures and when to keep your hands from interfering with your oral presentation.

(3) Practice relating to your mirror as you will have to relate to your audience, and especially to the TV camera or the Picturephone screen. Look straight at it as you would at a person to whom you are speaking directly. A self-conscious, inexperienced speaker is apt to shift his gaze, looking up at the ceiling or down at the floor, displaying his uneasiness. The picture your viewer should get of you is an affirmative one—a self-possessed executive who can face up to any situation.

Once you've passed the mirror test, you'll know you have it made.

Read Aloud

Reading aloud is recommended by most coaches and teachers of speech. Your wife and children are your best audience. Practice on them, or on any friends you can corral and whose judgment and criticism you respect. Poetry is ideally suited for this purpose, since the cadence and rhythm will encourage a speaking style that is not stilted or stereotyped. As Marianne Moore phrased it: "In a poem the words should be as pleasing to the ear as the meaning is to the mind."

By reading aloud:

(1) Your self-confidence is heightened, and your delivery will acquire an assurance, giving the proper emphasis to the meaning and significance of the words you are reading, and stressing the more important phrases and sentences.

(2) As a silent reader you may be inclined to gallop through the material at the rate of 600 words or more per minute, just to get the gist of the subject. But reading aloud, your tempo will of necessity have to slow down, averaging about 125 words per minute. You can then gauge your speech tempo for the best articulation and enunciation when you have to speak before an audience or into a microphone or tape recorder.

(3) Pronunciation of difficult words will no longer prove embarrassing tongue twisters. They will come naturally enough once you follow your dictionary's phonetic recommendations, and practice saying the words out loud until you have mastered accenting the proper syllables.

To Thine Own Self Be True

Impersonating a speaker you admire or imitating the voice and gestures of your favorite actor is courting disaster. Don't waste your creative energy pursuing the impossible. There was only one Winston Churchill who was able to obliterate his speech defect by his brilliant and colorful oratory. And only in a TV script can a Perry Mason shatter sedate court proceedings with a poker-faced denouement. Nor has anyone been able to duplicate the rich resonance of Franklin Delano Roosevelt's voice. Even if you are an overendowed mimic, your performance will still be a parody. Each individual has his own style, and that style should be cultivated and developed to fit his own personality, Centuries ago, in one of his oratorical declamations, Demosthenes stated: "A vessel is known by the sound, whether it is cracked or not; so men are proved by their speech, whether they be wise or foolish."

Your Total Image

Not all executives who will be expected to face an audience, who will appear on closed-circuit TV, or who will be seen on the Picturephone screen are endowed with that magic formula that makes stars out of actors and orators out of public speakers, the divine spark or the magnetic personality that commands attention the moment they make an appearance.

Nevertheless, you as an executive will have to project an image that should be pleasing to the eye, and, of course, capture and hold the audience's attention.

The total image you present will be the person your viewers will evaluate; they will admire you, listen to you, or dismiss you. In addition to the content of your message, there are several essential ingredients which will carry your public one way or another: your personality, your poise, your voice, your manner of presentation. But the first glimpse they will get of you, even before you utter a sound, is how you look and what you are wearing. On the surface this may sound inconsequential, even frivolous, but the cliché that "clothes make the man" still holds good. This is particularly true when you appear on the screen. Top management may be permissive about rumpled suits and a five o'clock shadow, but the TV camera and Picturephone screen are ruthless and critical judges.

Urbanity and elegance were just two of the elements that underlay the brilliant letters Lord Chesterfield wrote to his son, outlining the manners and standards to be pursued by a man of the world. At one point he wrote: "Take great care always to be dressed like the reasonable people of your age, in the place where you are; whose dress is never spoken of one way or another, as either too negligent or too much studied."

It is obvious, therefore, that the right-suited executive is a well-groomed person, whose clothing perferences are selected, of course, by his individual taste, local customs, and to some extent by the fashion look. The executive fashion look is the look of success. Establishment's yardstick is the well-tailored, right-fitting suit, the coordinated shirt and tie, dark socks, and polished shoes.

A Character in Search of a Script

(1) Preparation of your script in advance will be the difference between a good, tight, polished talk and a rambling discourse with the salient points lost in verbiage. Even if you are an expert in your field, articulate and glib, a script prepared and coordinated in advance will be a booster that will give potency to your address.

(2) Memorize your lines. Reading from notes is inadvisable. Often such reading is stilted and leaves your listeners uninspired. Moreover, the rustling of papers during your talk might drown out your words. The best posture is to look at your audience, rather than keep your head down to read from your notes. In the case of TV, look at your stand-in audience, that is, directly into the camera.

(3) Statistics and quotations are two types of written notes you may wish to have on hand. Such notes are best typed in double or triple space for reading ease, and preferably on cards, which are not apt to rustle in handling.

Finally, a bit of ego-massage for an executive with a low quotient in exhibitionism is helpful. A newly inducted citizen in McLuhanland might tuck away in his memory book this century-old adage of Thomas Carlyle's: "Alas the fearful unbelief is unbelief in yourself."

CLOSED-CIRCUIT TELEVISION AND PICTUREPHONE

Smile! You're on candid camera! Correction: You are on *two* candid cameras. If closed-circuit television isn't zooming in, then Picturephone is panning in for that close-up of you. Or both may be operating at the same time. And there is no escape. You're on view, whether you like it or not.

Robert Burns must have had his antenna turned into our century when he wrote: "Oh wad some power the giftie gie us to see oursels as others see us!" Which translated into modern Americanese simply means: "You'd better get with it, man. You may be caught with your psyche showing."

With exposure on closed-circuit TV as well as on Picturephone, an executive's already burdened dossier of performance qualifications will call for additional talents: notably the expertise of a polished actor. The executive will have to make like a star performer without benefit of a behind-the-scenes director. Should he fluff his lines or act out his own laugh-in show, there is no one to call "Cut" to save his face. Nor can he afford the indulgence of freezing in mute embarrassment or have an attack of self-consciousness that would make him stutter his lines and contort his face in anxiety.

At this rate, recruiters and personnel managers may be thrust into the role of casting directors. Potential executives may be rated not only on their professional business ability and experience but also on their photogenic possibilities and their talents as performers.

In-House TV

Closed-circuit television is management in the guise of Big Brother keeping an eye on you. This sophisticated audio-visual system is demonstrating aptitudes that cover the entire spectrum of industrial operations—training, selling, safety, surveillance, research, meetings, conferences, overall exchange of intracompany information, etc. In some organizations, every staff member is tuned in at one time or another, and in full view, from top management to the white-collar office worker, including every blue overalled employee in the shop or on the assembly line.

Even the company cafeteria is wired for sound and sight. While employees are munching their sandwiches and sipping their coffee, they are a captive audience. Top management is reporting on everything the company feels should be of interest to the employees: new techniques in training, product information, the corporation's profit-sharing plan, a gentle prod reminding them of the Community Chest Drive, as well as such morale buildups as the company-sponsored recreational programs.

In the executive's private office there is a cut-off and a tune-in prerogative. But most executives have to keep their closed-circuit TV in operation a great deal of the time. One drug company has installed closed-circuit TV screens in each supervisor's office to monitor the conveyor belts wherever there are ten or more operators working. In factories where safety hazards are involved every area is mirrored on the screens, which are stationed in strategic spots, especially in managerial offices.

Whatever the circumstances, an executive has to be on call and has to be primed to look and act his best. He has to be prepared to give an impromptu performance and ad lib without the benefit of a teleprompter to give him his cues.

For example, a top management official may want information that he would normally ask his secretary to get from you. Instead, with closed-circuit TV he tunes in on you. So don't let him catch you resting your feet on your desk. Or maybe seeing you thus might be an advantage. Railroad magnate Edward H. Harriman unexpectedly stopped by the office of one of his executives. He caught the man with his chair tilted back and his feet on his desk. The executive hastily straightened up, expecting the worst, only to hear Mr. Harriman say, "I'm glad you take time out to think."

Conceivably, too, the president of the company may suddenly decide to call a "sit-in-your-own-office" meeting. He can do so simply by turning on the switch, or he can buzz you and anyone else he wants to join in the confab.

Multidivision corporations are scrambling to install closed-circuit TV, since scattered company field offices and other buildings, even in remote locations, can be linked to the organization's network via mobile recordings and playback facilities.

A company official can be video-taped in his own office, hopefully keeping his stage fright under control as he acts out his message and says his piece. The tape can be duplicated in as many prints as are required for distribution to all company branch offices, which are equipped, of course, with playback units. Management, thereby, can break through space and time barriers by making personal appearances without leaving home base.

Intraorganizational conferences, too, are in for a new reevaluation and approach. Whether held in the same building, or streamlined to link the scattered holdings in any part of the country, the message is projected simultaneously. The president has his say; charts, diagrams, and new products are flashed on the screen; and other scheduled speakers make their entrances and exits on cue.

For the less affluent corporations, the industry has been quick to introduce rental systems. For example, an entire sales-promotion campaign can be video-taped in color or in black and white, using rented equipment. Even the services of professional actors are on occasion enlisted. They are rehearsed to talk and act like salesmen. However, there are salesmen who resent losing their personal rapport with their customers and resist any outside interference. In the final analysis, it is their individual style, their highly specialized spiel, and their personality that make the sales. They argue that they, too, in a sense are showmen, and they insist upon having a piece of the action.

Since prerecorded tapes can be edited, with adjustments and corrections inserted, any salesman or any executive can, electronically speaking, do his own stuff.

Nevertheless, anyone who is tagged for a special video tape recording should approach his role with the serious intent of a performer. The telecast may be destined for intracompany playback, or tapes may be widely distributed for customer orientation. Whether you are slated to be the star performer to plug your speciality, or fill in as a bit player for another departmental presentation, you must be sure of your lines and know how to take your cues like a pro. With closed-circuit TV running the gamut from job, sales, and management training to personnel relations, quality control, merchandising, sales promotion, and plant processing, more and more executives will be called upon to do their act and say their piece. Even an executive who is not overly endowed with a case of exhibitionism, will nevertheless wish for an encore; in fact, his job may very well depend upon a return engagement.

Picturephone

Picturephone is exactly what its name implies: "see-the-caller-who-sees-you-as-you-talk" instrument; the personalized audio-visual system that shortly may very well doom the ordinary telephone as a quaint, obsolete relic, of interest only to antique collectors.

You'll have to get used to the idea that in the very near future, any business associate in any part of the country will be able to dial your phone and tune you in. Not only will you be exposed to view—what you look like and how you dress—but even the interior of your office will show, probably revealing more about you and your work habits than you suspect. From here on it will be possible for persons in different cities in any part of the United States to converse face-to-face over telephone lines.

The system is Bell's brainchild. It operates on the same principle as the telephone or ordinary television set. After you depress the "on" button and hear the dial tone, you dial the necessary telephone digits. When you are connected, you can adjust the knobs on the control pad for the desired volume and picture clarity, making sure your tie is straight and face composed.

The system is still on probation in a test arrangement with Westinghouse executives, who are the star performers between New York and Pittsburgh. If, at the conclusion of what Bell terms their "trial and market study," the results indicate a green light, they will move into a full-scale program, offering Picturephone service to the business world at large. The latest plan is to introduce the service on a limited scale in the near future. The prognosis points to more than a million Picturephone (PTP) sets in use by early 1980, when you, the reader, are in your prime.

A user of PTP can obtain close-up or wide-angle views merely by zooming in electronically. When you are close-up on camera, your costar in another city will be able to read every nuance of expression while listening to your words. On the wide-angle view, participants can move about freely from side to side, motion with their hands, make dramatic gestures, and fulfill any histrionic ambitions they may have been keeping under cover.

Of course, there is always the possibility of a wrong-number rhubarb. The PTP dial system operates on the same principle as does the regular telephone, plus the screen for vision. This may offer a rich lode of material to the cartoonists and the jokemakers, but it is no laughing matter to the busy executive. An executive may answer his PTP ring and face an unfamiliar person on his screen. Should he discover his caller was merely a careless dialer, however, it is no invitation for the executive to begin displaying a snarling countenance or exploding with irritation. His bad manners will show to his disadvantage, and an irascible performance does not exactly convey a portrait of a self-possessed individual. Moreover, the wrong dialer might turn out to be a high official in another company, for who else besides high officials and other executives merit Picturephone installations, at least for the time being?

A notation a young executive might keep in his memory book is the fact that the trend is for top brass to dial their own telephone numbers. For example, President of CBS Dr. Frank Stanton is reputed to place his own calls and frequently answers his own telephone.

Though PTP is only a fledgeling, it has already been dubbed "the hot line" by executives who are less than enchanted with its demonstrated talents. They anticipate it with suspicion. As one executive put it: "It's like a surrealist nightmare with the watchful eye fixed upon you no matter how much you try to get away from it."

At Westinghouse, an official was quick to point out that the system has no similarity whatsoever to the Big Brother concept and that it is in no way a menace to privacy. If PTP is not actually Big Brother, it is certainly Little Brother doing his sibling best.

Conferences via PTP are no longer a speculative idea but a reality. Research and development are still in progress. But since 1964, regular commercial service has been in operation between PTP centers in New York, Chicago, and Washington, D.C. Although useful from a technical standpoint, the three-city hookup has provided limited measurement of the usefulness to customers of the service, since individuals have to make arrangements in advance and then go to the PTP centers to complete their calls. Nevertheless, the service in these locations has given some indication of its widespread potential. Multi-city conferences, while the participants are sitting cozily in their own offices, are making big, swelling waves for the future.

The "see-you-while-you-talk" possibility also has an international accent. As far back as 1935, a television telephone service was operated by the German Post Office between video-telephone centers in Berlin, Leipzig, Nuremberg, and Hamburg. In 1963, Pye Telecommunications, Ltd., exhibited a television telephone at the Business Efficiency Exhibition held in London. During the same year, reports were received from Italy and Japan of slow-scan video-telephone experiments. The Soviet Union also reported a public video-phone service using regular TV network facilities during nonbroadcasting hours.

These are smoke signals easily read: The American multilingual executive will be in great demand. It isn't too soon for a young executive with the burn to succeed to start taking refresher courses now, or digging out his college textbooks on foreign languages and brushing up on those French, German, Italian, or Spanish subjunctive verbs.

Managements of large American corporations are naturally keeping a close watch on Picturephone's development and progress. This is especially true within the managements of those corporations that have dependent or related companies, since among other talents, PTP service and the computer are like a happily mated pair. Corporations which have access to a computer can dial the computer and receive on the PTP screen such updated information as inventory, sales charts, and production schedules, as well as stock-market reports. A data set, developed at Bell Telephone Laboratories, links the PTP set to the computer. Using the "touch-tone" buttons, the user simply selects from a list of services the information he wants displayed. The computer's output is then translated by the data set and displayed on the Picturephone screen.

YOUR IMAGE

On the Screen

Even on the black and white screen, the big tube can be skittish about color and color tones. If closed-circuit TV is part of your company's equipment, here are some wardrobe tips that will help you project your image with professional finesse.

(1) The colored shirt, once taboo in Establishment circles, now has to be accepted as part of the executive uniform. This applies particularly to the screen. Large expanses of white are a strain on the TV camera, producing fade-out, glare, and other distortions. In fact, the colorful changeover in men's shirts can be attributed to TV's newscasters and performers, who have to wear them professionally and now sport them privately. Almost any colored shirt will look white on a TV screen, without causing a surrounding black halo. Light green or blue shirts are recommended, though professional directors and lighting experts are responding to the new deep tones, such as navies and chocolates. But for color TV, these shirts should be worn with a suit of contrasting color, and, of course, a dramatically colored tie.

(2) Black in large masses should be avoided, though a little black just for contrast is desirable. The camera is not versatile enough to capture black, either in clothes or objects, in excessive amounts. If the background where the telecast is being held is dark, then a light-colored suit is preferable. Of course, with a light background there is no problem. An executive with his mental and personal file well organized will keep a change of wardrobe in his office closet. With experience he will soon learn which combinations of colors, values, and materials will serve him best. This may throw his budget out of gear—mortgage payments on the house, installments on the new car—but it is up to him to decide which comes first.

(3) Jewelry, however modest, or for that matter, any metallic surface, presents a problem. A simple tie clasp is likely to reflect light so strongly as to be ringed with a black halo. The same applies to a signet ring. If the stone is large, it will

catch reflections and disturb the camera, especially if one is given to gesturing and using his hands to illustrate a point.

(4) Makeup for closed-circuit TV is not really necessary, but a little touch of pancake may add greatly to the total effect. Some of the smaller commercial TV stations that have been indifferent to using makeup have found that some of their distinguished guests appeared on the screen with glowing scalps or shiny noses, much to the chagrin of the "performers." In most instances, an executive's appearance on the screen will be a chest shot or a waist shot, in which case, his face has to be featured. Makeup will not make him look handsomer, but it will help him present a well-groomed, clean visage. (a) A high forehead or a balding scalp is apt to respond too enthusiastically to the camera, reflecting unwelcome glowing surfaces. Apply makeup right up to the hairline and, of course, on any bald spots. (b) Cake makeup is recommended rather than greasepaint. It is easier to apply and to remove, and it is much cooler. (c) Five o'clock shadow is no clock watcher. It may creep up on you at any hour of the day, and when you are least aware of it, it too will show on the screen. "Beard stick" is a greasebase solution, easily applied. (d) Too much makeup may cast you in the role of a comic, so don't be heavy-handed or lavish.

On the Picturephone

On PTP screens, there is no problem of any color distortion, halos, or shadows. Bell has developed a tube that is different from the regulation TV tube and is designed for "rugged use." An official source indicates that a good quality picture is transmitted even when the lighting is poor, and even tie clasps or other jewelry will not blind out the lens.

DANGEROUS QUIPS

Jokes may be hazardous to your executive posture. Like the stand-up comedians on television, who feed a mesmerized public with their sick-sick-sick humor, the business world has its own breed of would-be jokesters and pranksters. The company's closed-circuit TV cameras and equipment may prove irresistible to some high-spirited young executives. Certainly

PTP has limitless possibilities for fun and games. Take warning! *Don't do it*. Management is not as permissive as today's society appears to be. Nor is management receptive to practical jokes and undignified executive behavior. In fact, management has a pronounced allergy to such conduct.

7. Communication: The Written Word

We are a generation that looks and runs. We'd rather talk than write, and if we must write, we too often settle for a memo as telegraphic as Morse-code language. During the past several decades, letters worthy of being preserved for posterity are mourned as a lost art and a relic of our more leisurely days.

Today's letters, even the social and personal ones, are usually typewritten. They are shorter and more specific. Gone are the flowery phrases, the polished sentences. Instead, letters are business-like: simple, concise, precise, and to the point.

Yet, we are to a great extent a paper civilization. The larger the organization, the more it depends on an interchange of written information. Many companies supply memo pads to all members of their staff with boldly inscribed script: "Don't say it. Write it." Even with the increased practice of microfilming, corporate warehouses and other storage areas are jam-packed with voluminous stacks of papers: contracts, minutes of meetings, reports, carbon copies of letters, memos, and all the required paraphernalia for future reference. In a sense, these constitute the history of the company, and in a broader sense the romance of American enterprise in action.

An executive might bear in mind that the letter or report that he is writing may very well end up in the company's archives as a permanent record. What he is saying and how he is saying it should have relevancy and be worthy of his efforts and his brain sweat.

Alfred P. Sloan, Jr., president and chairman of the board of General Motors, received his industrial baptism while working for a struggling young firm called Hyatt Roller Bearing Company. A letter Mr. Sloan wrote to Henry Ford on May 19, 1899, soliciting business from him is still in the Ford archives.

A barometer indicating the significance of communication to the life stream of any company is the program of the American Business Communications Association. Its headquarters are at the University of Illinois in Urbana, and its membership includes distinguished professors, training directors, business executives, and consultants. The association deals with all phases of business communications—written, oral, and graphic. In addition, they publish a quarterly, *The Journal of Business Communications*. Regional meetings and national conventions are held periodically, enabling members and participants to meet and talk with leaders in the field.

These activities are indications of the increasing signposts pointing toward professionalism in writing business letters and reports.

A prominent consultant advised a group of executives: "Your letters should not be stilted. They should not stammer or stutter. Say what you have to say clearly and concisely, always expressing the goodwill of your company as well as your own." A little infusion of individuality never hurts and is likely to capture the interest of the person you are addressing. A good mind is revealed in a well-constructed letter as much as in a well-constructed speech.

Here are a few guidelines for good communication. They are equally applicable to letters, reports, or memos.

(1) Accurate, clear thinking. Know what you want to say; have your facts clearly outlined in your mind or on paper before you attempt to dictate or write.

(2) Avoid clichés like "It behooves me to say," "I take the liberty of suggesting," "pursuant to our discussion," "above mentioned," or any of the other tired old phrases. Say what you have to say as though you were talking directly to the person or persons you are addressing. Get right to the point with short, concise sentences.

(3) Don't try to dazzle your readers with your technical knowledge, unless you are writing to a colleague for whom these terms are part of his professional jargon. The average layman who is not familiar with your specialized vocabulary

will be baffled and doubtless annoyed that he is being placed at a disadvantage. It is a waste of your and your secretary's time and the company's money if what you are writing is not achieving the desired results. Your writing style should be simple, readable, and readily understood by a person of average intelligence.

(4) Do not write anything, certainly not a letter or an interoffice memo, while you are angry. Wait until you simmer down. What you write in fury you will regret in composure. An emotional upset impairs rational thinking. If you write a compromising message, it not only reflects unfavorably on you but remains a permanent document in someone's file or in the company archives.

Whenever Thomas Edison was angry, he sat down and wrote a scathing letter. But he never mailed it. He left it on his desk for a day or two, and then tore it up.

(5) Neglecting to answer a letter as soon as possible is a discourtesy. Neglecting to answer a business letter within a few days is bad business and a blemish on the company's good name.

Queen Elizabeth of England receives countless thousands of letters from all over the world. Nevertheless, each is read and answered, even the splotchy notes from children. The replies are always considerate and very polite. The Queen never signs letters or gives her autograph to anyone not known to the royal household. Four ladies-in-waiting attend to the correspondence, usually starting each letter with a statement like "I am commanded by the Queen," and signed "Yours sincerely" (Buckingham Palace prefers this complimentary close) with the name and title of the lady-in-waiting answering the letter. Unless it is a blatantly crank note, it will be answered.

BUSINESS LETTERS

Brevity

The letters are short, to the point, and courteous. Nietzsche said that he preferred "to say in ten sentences what others say in a whole book. The more you say, the less people remember. The fewer the words, the greater the profit."

Brevity is not necessarily synonymous with curtness. It need not eliminate a "thank you for your letter" or for the information sent. Nor does it have to be dehumanized, even if your correspondent is not personally known to you. A little infusion of friendliness and warmth doesn't hurt. Such letters are sure to be gratefully received.

The uncluttered, down-to-basics business letter, without trite and pretentious phrases, is the dynamic, positive way of getting your message across. Such a letter is also considerate and courteous, since it saves the reading time of the recipient, who doubtless is already sufficiently inundated with paper work. A brief letter is also profitable; it cuts down dictating and typing time, for which your secretary too will be grateful. The one-page letter is read at once, perhaps even on the run. The two-page letter is often put aside to be read if and when time permits.

Despite all the latest electronic innovations, letters still remain the indispensable tools in the everyday life of buisness. Good letters yield results; careless, poorly phrased, or verbose letters make no contribution to the company's image. In every letter you write, you are selling yourself, your products, and your company. So be natural. Just "talk" with the ease and confidence of a man who knows his business and who has developed an individual style.

Exactitude and Clarity

If you are not sure of your facts, don't put them in writing. Mistakes are costly; written mistakes can emblazon your name in management's hall of the infamous. An erroneous statement, a misplaced cipher, a misquoted price, and your innocent letter may stir up latent litigious compulsions in your correspondent and become Exhibit A in a disagreeable wrangle.

Before attempting to dictate or make a recording to be transcribed, the executive with an orderly mind will have before him the complete file of any previous correspondence. He will also keep handy price lists, account records, catalogues, and perhaps stock availability.

If you are in doubt about any fact, consult your superior. It will flatter him to know you are aware of his broader experience and he can guide you in the right direction.

Salutations—The Identity Ploy

No one enjoys anonymity or mistaken identity. A person likes to be called by his right name. A busy executive receiving a letter addressed to "Dear Sir" or "Gentlemen" can only assume that it is a circular letter and is likely to banish it to the circular file. If your correspondence is to have any impact upon the recipient, a little effort on your part, or your secretary's part, to obtain the name of the individual to whom the letter is to be addressed may prove a profitable expenditure of time.

Even if you are sorely tempted, try not to address a correspondent as "Dear Friend." If you don't know him, it's like slapping a stranger on the back. If you do know him, you owe him the courtesy of acknowledging his identity. Otherwise, he might assume that you have forgotten his name and you are taking the easiest way out.

A personal touch, which is becoming increasingly popular with managers writing a sales pitch, is to repeat the name of the addressee in the body of the letter ("If you want additional information, Mr. Stranger, please let me know").

Is She Miss or Mrs.?

When you write to a woman and you are not certain whether she is married or single, you are safest addressing her as "Ms." This form of address is now almost universally accepted and is favored by those who like to play it safe. Some married career women continue to use their maiden names for the purpose of identity. Those who prefer to use their married name sign themselves "Gloria Maddox Smith," but under the signature is typed "Mrs. Maxwell Smith." A business letter is often addressed to "Mrs. Gloria Smith," but this practice is not carried over into social life, where the correct address is still "Mrs. Maxwell Smith."

Watch out for the name that looks like "Miss" but is actually "Mr." or vice versa. This is especially true in England, where given names are apt to be interchangeable, such as "Evelyn," "Marion," "Sydney," "Leslie." An Englishman can become exceedingly John Bullish if he is addressed as "Dear Miss."

Spelling the Name

Some men may be merely annoyed when their names have been misspelled. Others have been known to be on the indignant side. No one likes to see his name distorted. It implies that the person addressing him regards him as of too little consequence, and he is justifiably affronted.

He may be "Mr. Smith" to you, but he is really "Mr. Smythe" when you write to him. And there are Eliotts who feel neglected if one *t* is left off, and there are Haskells who insist on the double *l*.

Given names are also sensitive areas, sometimes reflecting family pride and tradition. If a man spells his name "Alec," he won't relish being addressed as "Alex," and he may be equally touchy if his middle name or initial is not acknowledged. He may also feel deprived if you omit the "Jr." or only partially groomed if it is not specifically stated that he is Prescott R. Square III.

With our geographical boundaries shrinking and our trade expanding, the correct spelling and pronunciation of names are more important than ever. There are cultures in different parts of the world where the family name is not regarded merely as a matter of pride but as an honor above all other worldly possessions. A man conditioned from early childhood to the dignity and importance of his name would regard even a minor infraction as an insult.

In Great Britain there are many who are devoted to the hyphenated name, and it is bad form to abbreviate or shorten the name of "Mr. Proctor-Smedley." When writing to him, he is always "Dear Mr. Proctor-Smedley."

The real snag is that so many foreign names are jawbreakers, and the spelling is eccentric, to put it mildly. There are Ryszkiewiczs, Vladabotcheks, Kaihatsus, Mao Tchang-koos, Nguymen Cao Kys, and Abd-al-Rahmans, to name a few.

There is little consolation in remembering that foreigners probably have the same problems with our American names that we have with theirs.

Your Signature

Your secretary will, of course, type your full name and title at the close of the letter, but your John Hancock should be legible. The reference to a "John Hancock" signature is derived from the boldness and legibility of his autograph; this is a courtesy a modern executive might remember when he is scribbling his name, which is too often undecipherable and unreadable.

There may be occasions when you are not available and your secretary signs your letters for you. Even if she has learned to forge your signature to the very dot of an *i*, she must remember to add her own initials in writing. This is a safeguard in case there are any unexpected repercussions or questions asked. In large corporations where the legal department is on the premises, a steely eye is kept on this procedure.

Carbon copies of letters to be routed to others do not necessarily require a handwritten signature. Initialing the copies by hand, though, make it official, and adds that personal touch that is always appreciated.

THE INTEROFFICE MEMO

Company officials are fed up with too much talk and not enough action in regard to the breakdown or absence of proper communication within the organization. One of the roadblocks in the channels of good communication is the executive who plays the game with his cards too close to his chest. Whether he is nursing visions of himself as the old-time do-it-yourself tycoon who made it by his own secret formula; whether he harbors the executive-bugaboo of giving too much rope to his subordinates; or whether he is congenitally incapable of committing himself in writing or in speech, he stands in the way of productive performance and contributes to the frazzling of a sensitive corporate nerve center.

The interoffice memo by no means solves this knotty problem, but it does help to pass along instructions and assignments; it is a useful feedback confirming verbal decisions or informal discussions which require follow-up, and just as important it siphons FYI (for your information) material to the required departments.

Companies of all sizes and categories have specially designed memo forms which meet their organizational setup, many of them custom-tailored to encourage or even coerce executives to say it in writing.

The most commonly used form is imprinted with all the essentials, requiring only filling in the necessary data and following with the message. Executives like these forms because they are convenient and speedy. Because they come in triplicate, it saves time. The executive has a copy for himself, and the third is for the record.

Messages can be typed or handwritten, but should be handwritten only if one's penmanship is clear and readable. It's an imposition to expect anyone, busy or otherwise, to attempt to decipher a scribbled scrawl.

One of the hidden advantages for a young executive is that having to write frequent interoffice memos, he masters the skill of expressing himself fluently and with a certain flair and style. Like musicians who practice every day to keep in tune and authors who keep journals to sharpen their words, the continuous flow of memo-writing teaches a person to say in precise, accurate terms exactly what he has on his mind; he learns to put his words to work for him, to say what he has to say without any fuss or flourish.

The writer of the memo is directing his message to a specific audience. Knowing his reader, writing directly to him, actually as though he were talking to him, he gets into the habit of writing with authority and assurance—a ready-made practice program that meets the needs of an executive whose professional expertise is dependent upon how skillfully he masters the art of communicating.

Not all executives can be inveigled into using the memo forms, jiffy or otherwise. One vice-president of a chain of department stores has a mental block about putting anything in writing. He gives his instructions verbally. When, as can sometimes happen, there is a foul-up, he assumes a righteously indignant stance at the inefficiency of his department. In self-protection, his assistant has taken to sending him memos confirming all instructions. The veep is not taking this maneuver in good grace. He is grumbling: "Stop flooding me with memos. I haven't got the time to read them." It's a toss-up who is going to win out.

8. The Executive Fashion Look

In the jargon of management consultants, a man's entrance through a door—the first impression he makes—is the "threshold effect." It determines whether his general appearance will or will not match the executive suite.

In *The Pyramid Climbers* Vance Packard asserts that "numerous men who have spent years appraising executives, speak freely, and often unexpectedly, of the importance of appearance. One gets the impression that physical appearance is becoming especially important to executive success and that it becomes especially important for the promising younger executives who are getting up near the peak of the larger corporation pyramids—and who hope to be regarded as having all the ingredients of a 'successful package.' "

The clothes an executive wears are his personal statement of identity. They speak volumes about him—as much as his educated vocabulary or his gift for repartee. They are his own sales package selling *him*.

The executive "uniform" may no longer be the gray flannel suit, but it closely resembles it in its conservative style and button-down look. Big business still favors the white and the pastel-colored shirts, though darker and brighter solids, discreet checks, and bolder stripes are becoming more acceptable. A group of vice-presidents of a prestigious bank have recently conspired to wear their brightest-colored shirts to the office one day a week in an effort to lower the resistance of their immediate superiors.

The regimental striped tie is still very much in evidence; the hand-painted abstract designs and neckerchiefs have been known to raise the hackles of even a mild-tempered over-lord.

Slowly but surely, the Ivy look is being inched out of the League. One contributing factor is the multifaceted international exchange of executives. Traveling abroad, the American businessman, conditioned to inconspicuous conformity, considers it to his advantage to blend in with the foreign scene. Apparently, foreign executives who come to America are like-minded. There is a lively export-import exchange of men's fashions among the major designers from New York, London, Paris, Rome, Madrid, and other capitals.

The first signs of liberating men's sartorial regimentation had originally come from Paris, with a slimmed-down, waist-hugging longer jacket, which has since been imitated throughout the world and remains a best-seller in shops all over the United States.

In England, Savile Row continues to be traditional, holding the line on the gentlemanly gentleman look, but among the new designers, the longer shaped jackets and trousers with diagonally cut, cuffless bottoms are gaining acceptance.

Nor have the American designers been caught napping. Their specified target is the international businessman for whom they create suits with an adventurous use of fabrics, but, nevertheless, hewing to the conservative silhouette, the single-breasted style predominating. These are destined for the American market, as well as for foreign export.

Of course, the international style signals may sometimes be misread. Witness the well-meaning intentions that boomeranged when an American oil executive invited two visiting Saudi Arabians to his home for dinner. The host and hostess were outfitted in the latest boutique caftans, while the guests appeared impeccably suited in the best British tradition.

WHEN IS A FAD NOT A FASHION?

A discerning executive should know how to discriminate between fashion and fad. He need only be guided by the simple basic fact that good taste in appearance is necessary if he wants to command respect. Being in style does not necessarily mean wearing the latest caprice concocted by a dilettante designer whose acquaintance with the average business executive may not be even on a nodding basis.

An executive's appearance must be supported by management's acceptable image, and his own projection of himself in his chosen career. No executive who values his job can afford to deviate from the corporate pattern with any brazen fashion innovations that would displease management. Industry, for all its exuberant acceptance of the most sophisticated technological inventions, is not quite as avant-garde when an executive's appearance does not conform to the standard notion of the norm. A dapper, style-conscious individual may get away, without too much comment, with minor variations, such as the width of the trouser legs, the shape and width of the jacket lapels, or the slant of the pockets. Our industrial society is still dominated by the conservative older generation, whose tacit standards must be respected. Eventually, the younger executives will replace the old guard, when it will be their turn to be critical of the next generation. But until that time, youth must harness frivolity and defer to the judgment of its ranking superiors.

Some corporations have been known to issue directives and guidelines outlining the "total image" they wish their employees, especially their executives, to project. This has sometimes stirred up resentment and rebellion.

One internationally famous corporation, equally famous for its paternalistic attitude, allegedly enforced strict dress regulations upon all its employees. Sport jackets, colored shirts, and argyle socks are only a sampling of the taboos allegedly decreed by the conformism-oriented management. Pipe smokers were presumably regarded as dreamers rather than workers, and therefore pipe smoking on any of the company premises was also supposedly discouraged.

However, inquiries among the various executives of the corporation brought amused disclaimers. Further inquiries revealed that at one of their research plants tucked away in a wooded area, the scientists and the laboratory technicians ignore the executive syndrome. They wear shorts and no tie during the hot summer months. And as for the secretaries, their current dilemma is whether they should wear miniskirts or pants, with the miniskirted brigade thus far winning out.

THE INTELLIGENT MAN'S GUIDE TO GOOD GROOMING

As They Like It

An executive should never wear anything that tests his courage. If he does not feel that a certain style is for him, he should reject it.

Whatever the current fashion look might be, if it does not suit his individual style or fit his particular proportions, it is not for him. It is a well-known fact that self-confidence and poise are given an extra charge when one *knows* one's appearance is up to standard.

Your clothes should be an extension of *you*. They should feel comfortable and they should look comfortable. If they are not comfortable, they become an armor and cease to be appropriate wearing apparel.

Good appearance is the first step toward capturing attention. A survey was recently conducted among leading executives of the nation's largest companies. They were asked what they noticed first when they saw a man in a business setting. The replies were startling: 79 percent noticed a badly knotted tie; 72 percent noticed a lack of proper crease in jacket or trousers; and 59 percent said that they immediately noticed a poorly fitted suit. Obviously, what is seen of a person at first glance is his outfit. Clothes are crucial in forming the all-important first impression.

Your wardrobe is not a luxury but an investment. Your investment will pay off if your executive survival wardrobe conforms to top management's concept of inconspicuous traditional neatness. The image you want to present is that of responsibility, respectability, and trust. You cannot achieve this by wearing the clothes of a nonconformist. You would only be an anti-hero to your company, and invite a frowning, alienating reception from the other members of your organization and your customers.

Business will probably always carry the banner of tradition and conservatism in clothing, if for no other reason than that clothes should not be so conspicuous as to detract attention from the business at hand, and they should at all times be appropriate to the situation.

Your pace will be faster up the escalator of success if you have that well-pressed look. One secret ingredient is, if possible, to select suits tailored from crease-resistant material— certain to add a layer of security for the traveling or even commuting executive.

A sartorial offense some executives commit is to carry their "file cabinets" in their pockets, producing bulges which crumple the suit and distort the silhouette. Remember, the attaché case is still an executive's best friend.

Of course, there have been and still are men in the business and professional fields who follow no rules, dressing as they please and nevertheless managing to rise high. The famous Clarence Darrow, lost in his world of law, often appeared in disheveled clothes. When a group of reporters heckled him about it, he quipped: "I go to a better tailor than any of you and pay more money for my clothes. The only difference between us is that you probably don't sleep in yours!" Even if Clarence Darrow got away with it, you, the executive, may not do so. Also, it is easier to build for success without adding stumbling blocks.

Though the old-time shoeshine boys toting their boxes of polish and brushes from office to office are rapidly disappearing, the executive with pride in his appearance will wear shoes that are shined and in good shape. Unless, of course, he is the old John D. Rockefeller who could afford to overlook the finer niceties of dress. In his later years Mr. Rockefeller became attached to a comfortable but badly battered pair of shoes. He insisted on wearing them when he landed in England, in spite of his valet's objections and a polite suggestion that he change into a pair of newer and more presentable shoes, more fitting to a gentleman of Mr. Rockerfeller's standing and wealth. "Stop fussing," he interrupted. "In England nobody knows who I am!" On his arrival back in this country, he again insisted on the same pair of shoes. He hushed his valet's objections with: "Stop worrying. me—everybody here knows who I am anyway!"

The important thing to remember about clothes is the manner in which you wear them. A well-groomed man conveys an air of poise and casualness, and above all, self-confidence. It is the posture, the grace of carriage, that spells the signature of a debonair executive.

Evening Clothes

"A black tie," for a company function means that the evening will be more formal, perhaps more important, and probably more ceremonious. There is something about wearing a dinner jacket that can spark even the dourest personality into a sense of euphoria and anticipated festivity. The occasion may be a company banquet, presentation ceremony, formal entertainment of customers, a theater party, or any number of other company events.

If management considers the function important enough, it is incumbent upon the young executive to present himself looking his formal best. If you are not certain whether the evening requires a black tie, it is better to inquire. If you have no way of finding out in advance, you will feel more comfortable if you appear in a dark business suit rather than be the only person wearing formal attire.

It is interesting that a change into formal dress changes the person's manner, his attitude, the "way he walks and the way he talks," Because the undercurrent is social, the young executive can have a field day relating, impressing, and enchanting.

If there is a good deal of uniformity in men's daytime clothes, there is certainly much more in men's evening apparel, and the mark of distinction is primarily in the fit. The range of style and color variation is narrow, but there is a promise in the air to let the accoutrement fit the gala time.

Still timidly, but the colors are tiptoeing into men's evening clothes—midnight blue, maroon, and various off-black shades; cautious color touches here and there, and even shirt ruffles for the younger Beau Brummels. The peacock era? Perhaps. But will it ever spread to the solemn halls of business and industry?

Sampson's Dilemma—"Hair Apparent"

The new-style barber-shop quartet is singing: "Why can't a man let his hair down?"

The length of a man's hair is certainly not an indication of his masculinity or his business ability, but it may expose him as an extremist, an unwelcome advocate in the world of business.

In ancient times men cut their hair ceremonially as an offering to Hercules, a fitting tribute to a god capable of performing extraordinary feats of strength. Today, almost all extraordinary feats are performed through advanced technology, leaving man to seek other mischief in his pursuit of identity.

The under-thirty take-over among the "fast-money boys" has dotted the industrial landscape with young men sporting somewhat long hair, though no longer than a fringe sweeping the collar line. This is as much as big business has resigned itself to accepting.

Even the most advanced men's hair stylists warn that longer hair is not appropriate for all men. As one Hollywood taste-setter phrased it: "No one thing will look good on all people. The same applies to hair styles as applies to a pear-shaped man wearing tight-fitting pants and a shaped jacket, a short man in a long Edwardian coat, or a man with no forehead with hair hanging down onto his face."

The important thing to remember about wearing longer hair is that it requires more care, more frequent shampooing, and daily brushing. For the thinning head of hair and the hairless, there is a lively selection of wigs and toupees to cater to the increasing concern and pride men are beginning to show in their appearance.

The barriers that condemned the male of the species to a drab and colorless appearance are being lowered. The peacock is coming into his own. He can now flaunt his crest and spread the colors that nature originally meant for him.

The battle of the beard is a hair-raising problem. It is being fought on many fronts, with the older generation standing firm on the clean-shaven look. But members of the younger generation are sprouting luxuriant hirsute speciments, pointing out that from time immemorial the beard was considered by almost all nations as a sign of strength and manhood.

Someone who obviously had nothing better to do figured out that the average man scrapes away 27½ feet of whiskers in almost 3,350 hours, or 140 days of shaving time.

George Bernard Shaw's favorite beard story dates to the time when he was a small boy watching his father shave. He asked him: "Daddy, why do you shave?" His father looked at his son for a full minute, then said: "Why the hell do I?" With that, he threw down his razor and never shaved again.

As far back as ancient Egypt, when kings were regarded as

children of the gods, for ceremonial occasions the royal personages would wear thin lozenge-shaped false beards, well curled and always perfumed. For centuries, the setting of styles for growing beards continued to be a royal prerogative. If the king wore one, the subjects followed. When Philip V ascended the Spanish throne, loyal courtiers removed their beards, because the king was unable to grow one.

Beards came into disfavor in the early part of the twentieth century, when it was thought that only dangerous revolutionaries and anarchists sported them. In a sense history is repeating itself. Among some of today's youthful activists and objectivists, the beard is a sign of protest. Nevertheless, in the creative fields, beards are continuing to sprout and flourish— trimmed, pruned, and shaped with topiary inventiveness. Actors and other public figures are usually the trailblazers.

But in the sedate canyons of finance, only the portraits of the founding fathers are permitted to wear their long beards with no frowning objections on the part of the presiding denizens. Some of the younger executives, having gone through a transitional stage of lengthening their sideburns millimeter by millimeter are now swinging back to a greater exposure of the face. Lamb-chop and mutton-chop sideburns are no more. Among the devil-may-care contingent, however, many continue to flaunt mustachios with luxuriant handlebars and with an occasional 1970's version of the old goatee. As to the hair, according to Vidal Sassoon, internationally known authority for hair styling, "The trend now is toward a more manageable length covering the ears and either touching or coming slightly over the collar. The sloppy, tousled look is a thing of the past." Yet young executives are still apt to warn their hair stylists not to trim their hair too short.

9. A Company Is Known by the Men It Keeps

THE CONGLOMERATES

Mixing business with pleasure has become an integral part of the corporate life style, whether on the company's premises during the day or elsewhere after hours. As one executive put it, "Nothing is too good for our visiting firemen."

The conglomerates and their multiple acquisitions of big and small companies on the national as well as international scene have precipitated the shuttling back and forth of the new executive "cousins," both titled and untitled, distributors, customers, consultants, legal counselors, and so on.

The business policy issues are debated, argued, and litigated in the privacy of the corporate board room, the executive dining room, or the president's office. Sometimes these negotiations take days, weeks, and months. There must be time out for lunch and dinner. As a rule, provisions are made for evening and weekend entertainment not only for the visitors but, in many instances, for the wives who accompany their husbands.

CORPORATE LUNCHEON AND DINING FACILITIES

Office planners are a comparatively new breed of interior designers. They use multisyllable words to create "environmental control" as a corporate tool for personnel well-being.

Expanding organizations accept this brand of environmental thinking with a rider—a new-style concept of the on-the-premises eating facilities for top brass all the way down to the "troops." This is not benevolence but hard-core thinking, since creature comforts shape personnel performance in terms of the latest corporate catchword, human relations.

Providing accessible, confortable luncheon quarters in company dining rooms has many obvious cumulative advantages. Not the least is the build up of goodwill to encourage staff members to feel that they belong to one big happy family. The executive dining room in particular is inverted altruism, which benefits the organization as much as it does the executive. By providing luncheon facilities on the premises, the three-hour, alcohol-drenched restaurant sessions are by-passed, since most corporations prohibit the serving of intoxicating beverages on company property.

In most instances, the chef, the kitchen staff, and the waiters are company employees. Otherwise, the cuisine and control of the kitchens are concessions under the supervision of experienced caterers. Protocol is unwritten but strictly observed as to which level in the hierarchy is eligible to use which facility, and whether guests are welcome.

The number of dining areas varies with the size of the corporation. In larger corporations, in the majority of cases, the dining facilities for executives and employees fall into five categories.

(1) The private dining room for officers and members of tlhe board and their guests.

(2) The executive dining room which is exclusively for the use of top-level executives, with the cutoff point varying according to the policy of the individual corporation.

(3) The executive dining rooms with an open-door policy.

(4) The junior executive dining room.

(5) The company cafeteria.

Each dining facility is distinguished by its own set of rules, declared or otherwise.

The Private Dining Room

The private dining room is the sanctum sanctorum for top management and their guests only. In the newly constructed buildings it is generally located in the penthouse or other upper regions of the corporation's quarters tucked away out of sight and sound of the work-a-day hubbub.

Decoratively speaking, the private dining room is usually regal without being ostentatious. Even if the executive offices are starkly modern, the private dining room has a traditional look, doubtless to inspire confidence and not to overawe any visiting dignitary.

Actually, these private dining rooms are showcases to entertain visiting tycoons, or a rajah who wishes to invest his weight in gold. Here a gourmet lunch, served in surroundings that are a feast for the eye as well as for the digestion, may very well prove to be a selling tool to convince the toughest client.

Recently, an aviation equipment corporation turned its private dining room into a hospitable haven for a team of British bankers who had come to the United States to negotiate with the company. A directive was sent by the president of the American corporation to all top-level executives informing them that tea would be served promptly at four o'clock in the private dining room for the duration of the Englishmen's visit. No business was to be discussed during the tea break. The president's secretary acted as hostess. She knew that most Englishmen take milk with their tea, and she also put in a goodly supply of English tea biscuits. The tea party not only had a salubrious effect upon all but resulted in a long-term mutually beneficial relationship.

Some board chairmen and presidents of corporations are known to forgo the cloistered atmosphere of the private dining room when they have no luncheon guests at hand. They prefer the executive dining room, wherein an informal exchange with officers and other top management officials provides a cross-fertilization of ideas and feedback—a helpful, nourishing luncheon session for all concerned.

For the time being the door to the private dining room is closed to the young executive, but he is flirting with Dame Fortune in the hope that he will entice her to open that door wide enough for his triumphant entrance and perhaps his eventual take-over. His chances are much greater if he touches the knob gently, walks cautiously, and speaks in polite terms. His suave conduct may be one of the contributing factors oiling the machine that will pave his way toward his ultimate goal.

The Executive Dining Rooms

The prevailing domain where peerdom reigns is the executive dining room. Low-keyed elegance, comfort, chef-inspired cuisine, and often printed menus are all part of the scene.

Public-held companies prefer to keep these executive dining rooms under wraps—if possible. Stockholders, with their single-minded concern that the company exists primarily to make money and more money for them, might regard a handsome, elegant dining room as a waste of profits. Many stockholders are unaware of the mental and physical wear and tear on the average executive; they do not understand that a quiet dining room on the premises is actually a time-and-health saver, and that the higher the salary, the greater the executive's responsibilities, and the more he needs a quiet place in which to relax.

The dining room exclusively for top-level executives generally has tables accommodating two or four for cozy, confidential interdepartmental confabs, and large tables for six, eight, or twelve for the larger get-togethers.

Lunch is generally served from 11:30 to 1:30, though some dining rooms remain open until 2:30. No reservations are necessary, since an individual executive establishes his habitual eating hour and, through a curious process of thought transmission, each executive's favorite table and chair are regarded as his own.

Lower-echelon executives and outside guests are not welcome, since such intrusion would inhibit freedom of discussion and hinder the cross-fertilization process, a current obsessive phrase in corporate dialogue.

Rarely, and only rarely, is a lower-echelon executive granted the privilege of entering these sacred portals. On an occasion when there is an all-day meeting and time is of the essence, the discussions are carried over into the luncheon period and are continued in the executive dining room, where the junior executives are invited to join the group.

The executive dining room with open-door policy is more prevalent among the nontraditional neocorporations. These have less rigid acceptance rules, and outside guests are allowed. Yet, here, too, bureaucracy prevails and protocol must be observed. All level executives are privileged to use the facilities. The rooms are decoratively impressive, since important clients and out-of-town visitors are welcome to enjoy a taste of corporate hospitality. The seating arrangements usually allow for groupings of two to twelve. There are also private rooms for luncheon meeting sessions, which are equipped with hot-plate buffet tables and other necessary appliances.

The use of the executive dining rooms by young executives is a privilege and not a right. There are undeclared, unwritten rules that are inviolable.

(1) Some corporations require that all the executives make reservations in advance; others require prior notice only when outside guests are expected. In either case, you would be well advised to check with the steward to make sure that no one of top management is having luncheon with clients, especially if a junior executive's presence might not be acceptable.

(2) If you have invited a guest, and the company policy does not permit the serving of alcoholic drinks on the premises, mention this casually to your prospective visitor *before* making reservations. The guest's metabolism might require a drink or two, and he might prefer a restaurant with a bar.

(3) Be selective about the guest you invite to lunch in the executive dining room. The guest must be important enough to the company to warrant this privilege.

(4) You may be tempted to endow an outside friend with a bogus title and inflated references just to bring him to the executive dining room and impress him with the company you keep. Don't do it. The risk isn't worth it. Top management has a limited tolerance for youthful arrogance or pranks. Many companies keep a guest book for visitors to sign. A questionable signature may invite some unpleasant inquiries.

(5) Your guest may be an important client who knows about the executive dining room. If for one reason or another it is not available, do not substitute the regular employees' dining room. His sense of status may be offended. You may or may not wish to explain the circumstances, but in either case you should take him to one of the better restaurants in the neighborhood.

Junior Executive Dining Room

The indoctrination by industrial psychologists has awakened corporate thinking to a realization that junior executives, who are hopefully the future managers destined to infuse new blood and contribute toward creative progress for corporate survival, need a certain amount of coddling and wet-nursing.

Forward-thinking corporations instruct their office planners to have space allocated to dining areas for junior executives.

These are generally functional rather than decorative. To some extent they serve the same purpose for which the higher-echelon dining rooms have been created: to give the younger men a chance to get to know each other and to exchange views and ideas which may benefit the company.

Tables are arranged to seat four or more, and usually no guests may be invited.

The Company Cafeteria

White-collar snobs are losing their advantage if they bypass the company cafeteria. In the giant corporations, it is no longer an antiseptic, tray-jostling convenience for the personnel low on the totem pole.

The same thoughtful and considered attention that the office planners lavish on executive dining rooms are reflected in the company cafeterias, which are designed for the maximum convenience and comfort of the employees.

Many company cafeterias are open for breakfast as well as for lunch. It is not unusual for an executive vice-president or a general manager of a subsidiary to share a breakfast table with a junior executive, a factor not to be overlooked by a young man with the burn to succeed.

In suburbia and exurbia, where the company cafeteria may be the only food-dispensing convenience, even the president and the chairman of the board line up with their trays along with the rest of the staff.

There is a degree of corporate pride taken in the quality of food served in the cafeteria. If not quite up to the Brillat-Savarin standard, it is nevertheless good, solid American cuisine, with prices kept to a minimum.

In the newly constructed cafeterias, with the latest technological innovations, conveyor belts are installed. These are to facilitate housekeeping, and lunchers are expected to place their trays and soiled dishes on the belt, which quickly conveys them out of sight and into the kitchens. No rubbish or crumpled napkins are left on the tables.

Guests are permitted in some cafeterias, especially in outlying areas. However, in the metropolitan centers, particularly where company cafeterias have earned a high reputation for pleasing decor, good food, and nominal prices, outsiders are not admitted. In the large corporations, guards are posted at the door, and employees are obliged to show their company identification cards before they are permitted to enter.

10. Where the Action Is

Entertaining a client or a customer strictly for business reasons has become commonplace; it is routine. Luncheon meetings are a pleasant way of transacting business.

A young executive might be cum laude in business administration, but his post-graduate work would be considerably enhanced if he got to know where the action is: which restaurants serve the best boeuf à la mode and where you can get Cantonese as opposed to Mandarin cuisine; which place is bouncy and gay and where the latest underground bistro is located.

RESTAURANT LUNCHEONS

When a guest accepts your invitation to lunch, it is polite to query him if he has any food preferences. He may detest French food or he may just be in the mood for good old American roast beef and potatoes. He might also suffer from diabetes, executive ulcers, or be a victim of certain food allergies. Businessmen are understandably reluctant to reveal that they are not 100 percent physically fit. Giving your guest the choice of food is a thoughtful and courteous thing to do.

Once you know the kind of food your guest would like, give him a choice of restaurants. If you've done your homework, you ought to know two or three good places you can suggest that would satisfy his gastronomical tastes.

If some dire emergency arises and you have to break the appointment (and only something *unavoidable* should compel you to break a business luncheon appointment), there is but one right way of doing it—you telephone your guest yourself. If you are ill or cannot possibly do it, then try to get someone in your department who is on a comparable level to speak for you. Don't leave this important task to your assistant or secretary. This dooms it to a polite dismissal. A personal explanation is more meaningful and the only courteous way of handling such a situation.

On the day of the luncheon have your secretary telephone the restaurant to reserve a table. Have her tell the maitre d' that "it is important for Mr. Smith to have a good table." There is something that adds to the stature of an executive who, when he enters a restaurant with his guest, is shown immediately to a good table without having to wait in line. Also he will get much better service if the maitre d' recognizes him as *the* Mr. Smith. It is customary for the maitre d' to be rewarded with an honorarium slipped to him as unobtrusively as possible. He will be sure to remember your name again. The amount varies from a mere pittance to an astronomical amount, depending on the type of restaurant, the frequency of your patronage, and the elasticity of your expense account.

If your guest has been only a telephone voice and you do not know what he looks like, it would be wise for you to come to the restaurant earlier and give your guest's name to the maitre d', who will escort him to your table as soon as he arrives. Both you and your guest will be saved the embarrassment of scouting around trying to recognize each other.

"What will you have to drink?" is one of those "walking-on-eggshells" questions. Henry L. Mencken, who referred to himself as "ombibulous" ("I drink every known alcoholic drink and enjoy them all"), had a few pertinent thoughts on the subject of drinking during working hours: "A man who has taken aboard two or three cocktails is less competent than he was before to steer a battleship down the Ambrose Channel, or to cut off a leg, or to draw up a deed of trust, or to conduct Bach's B minor Mass; but he is immensely more competent to entertain at a dinner party, or to admire a pretty girl, or to hear Bach's B minor Mass."

If your guest is a nondrinker, he will of course refuse your offer. If he is minding his manners, he should suggest to you that if you feel like having a drink, just go ahead and order one.

He may neglect to tell you that he is on the wagon, or he may be a weight-watcher, or again he may be suffering from the occupational ulcer and cannot have a drink. But if you are a drinker and like to fortify yourself with one before lunch, it is perfectly correct to ask if he would mind, and suggest his joining you with a tomato juice or some nonalcoholic aperitif. However, if your guest refuses a drink for religious reasons, you may wish to show respect for his beliefs and forgo a drink.

If you are not drinking for one reason or another, mention this to your guest *before* he orders a drink, but insist that he go right ahead and order it. Don't embarrass him by letting him order a drink and then inform him that you're on the wagon. Some individuals object to drinking by themselves, nor is a guest likely to feel comfortable imbibing while his host abstains. Order for yourself a clam juice or something and drink along with him.

Why don't you want a drink? The most acceptable excuse, which every businessman understands, is the ulcer game. The one excuse you should avoid is to tell your guest that a drink at lunch makes you logy or that you have important work to do that afternoon and you have to be on the alert. You'll embarrass your guest and make him feel guilty, or worse, make him feel he ought to be on the alert, too.

One nondrinking executive handles this problem with aplomb. When his guest orders a drink, he orders a Virgin Mary or a Jane Collins. Waiters and bartenders understand the message: a Virgin Mary is tomato juice less vodka and a Jane Collins is tonic without gin. Sometimes he orders a Scotch highball with soda on the side, just to indicate that he's not a square. As the ice is diluting the Scotch, he sips the soda out of another glass while his guest is enjoying *his* drink.

Formerly, etiquette required that the guest inform the host what he would like to eat, and the host would then instruct the waiter. But developing manners bypass these formalities. Men are more comfortable when they do their own ordering. Women executives, who in a social situation may turn to their hosts and give their orders, will often at a business luncheon give their own orders directly to the waiter.

WHEN A WOMAN EXECUTIVE PICKS UP THE TAB

Gone are the days when a man considered his chivalry at stake when a woman executive paid for his lunch, though he must have known that he was actually a guest of her company and that the tab was an expense-account item.

Curiously enough, some top-management officials react with sportive amusement to the career-woman-who-pays bit. A female industrial psychologist relates that the president of a utility company, whenever he comes to town, telephones and says: "How about buying me lunch? I'm hungry." He gets a bang out of watching her sign the check; and when they retrieve his hat and coat, he insists that she tip the hat-check girl, too. "If you're going to treat me, you've got to go all the way."

Another woman executive tells about a bank manager whom she had invited to lunch, frankly for a brain-picking session. When she signed the check, he thought it was the most amusing thing that had ever happened to him. "I've always wanted to be a gigolo," he told her, "and now I know how it feels. Invite me for lunch again, won't you?"

By now waiters in most restaurants are sophisticated and experienced enough to recognize when a career woman is the hostess at a luncheon, and generally they give her the check.

Most executives use credit cards or charge accounts. Comptrollers of corporations prefer these evidences of legitimate business expenses. It is a special convenience for executive women when they hostess a luncheon or a dinner for men. It avoids their making a public display of counting out bills and groping for coins, while their guests put on an appearance of embarrassed indifference.

Remnants of chivalry still cling to many men, and acts of social courtesy are intrinsic and habitual. But women executives are inclined to be ladies in a hurry and all too often do not give their business escorts the opportunity to exercise their gallantry. It is an almost automatic reflex for a man to assist a woman with her coat. But many a woman executive will slip out of her coat and throw it over the back of a chair, often ignoring the man's effort to be helpful. The same applies to doors. It is usual for the woman to precede the man as they leave the restaurant. She is apt to pull the door open before the man has had a chance to reach for the knob.

These are small male courtesies but they add up to the niceties that transform the rules of etiquette into a pleasing pattern of behavior.

It is a rare man so gauche as to feel that in dealing with a woman executive he has to act the role of a Don Juan.

Women executives take their jobs with the same serious, competitive attitude as do men. It is embarrassing and disturbing for a woman executive who has arranged a luncheon to discuss business to be drawn into a battle of the sexes.

AFTER DARK

Evening entertainment for visiting executives, both male and female, is a serious part of corporate business.

Today, the corporate network with its complexes of acquisitions, mergers, assorted mills, plants, branch offices, and franchises throughout the country imposes a concern not only for its own plane-hopping executives but for the care and entertainment of visiting customers, distributors, clients, and suppliers.

Rank is a determining factor as to which resident executive is expected to do the honors for the guests. Generally, top management takes care of the top echelon, and so on down the line with each echelon taking care of its own.

Many executives recognize that off-the-job activities in a congenial atmosphere may prove more significant than the cut-and-dry negotiations conducted in the office or in the conference room. The eighteenth hole on the golf course still remains a significant spot to consummate a deal with a hearty handshake.

COMPANY COUNTRY CLUBS AND
HOTEL SUITES

There is nothing new about a corporation owning its own country club, ostensibly for the recreational pleasure of its employees. Corporations have been doing this for decades, and coincidentally, using the club facilities as status conveniences to accommodate out-of-town visitors. Similarly, in metropolitan areas the company hotel suite, which is usually reserved for the exclusive use of the company's own management and VIP guests, continues to be accepted practice.

Today, coast-to-coast commuting of executives has become routine. The anxiety-ridden, uptight executive has become a cliché of our generation. Traveling, away from his family, catching planes, adjusting to different time zones, and making the best of a strange city, all add to his pressures.

Progressive management has taken a cool look at the problem. Many companies have established permanent accommodations for the creature comforts of their traveling men, as part of their organizational and operational setup. This is by no means paternalism. It is realistic corporate thinking.

The same facilities may also be used for out-of-town customers, distributors, consultants, and other business visitors.

Companies which do not own their own country clubs make arrangements for permanent guest privileges at clubs in the vicinity of their plants.

A new twist is renting a "summer house" or a series of rooms in suburban beach areas. For the duration of the guest's stay, this is his home, and his privacy is respected.

Due to the shortage of suitable hotel accommodations in metropolitan areas, the sacrosanct company suite is no longer the exclusive haven for VIP's. The doors are now open to several ranks of visitors and corporate personnel.

Most of the companies maintain a hands-off policy. They provide the "living quarters," perhaps a rented car, and then leave the out-of-towner free to find his own amusements with companions of his own choice.

Not all corporations are as richly endowed with built-in talent as Rayette-Faberge, Inc. Cary Grant is one of their active directors. When he and President George Barrie are not flying the company executive jets to meetings, they relax in the company's plush headquarters in New York, a converted town house once owned by the Rockefellers.

11. Breaking Bread

THE RESIDENT EXECUTIVE WHO
HAS TO PLAY HOST

Executive initiative, enterprise, and imagination are valuable assets for the social scene as well as for the conduct of business.

There are some executives who consider entertainment of business clients a bore and an intrusion into their private lives. Nevertheless, no executive can afford to treat corporate entertaining as a chore. The majority of management members realize the value of corporate entertainment as a goodwill and profit builder.

Perhaps here, more than in any other area in a business relationship, tact and thoughtfulness leave a stamp of permanent effect. The element that tends to solve the thorniest of problems is the personal equation.

The care and feeding of visiting moguls and their retinues adds another dimension to an executive's responsibilities. His business know-how must be enhanced by his poise and his manners on the social scene. He has to demonstrate his tact and his social sense—knowing the right thing to do at the right time and at the right place for the individuals with whom he is dealing.

The executive's motto should be: Don't entertain unless you entertain the right way. And the right way does not have to be an elaborate celebration. Gone are the days when the host-company felt it had to indulge its business guests in personal amusements. Today, a good dinner in a de luxe restaurant or hotel, and perhaps theater or a nightclub afterward, is sufficient in most cases.

Like any well-planned social occasion, thought must be given to the admixture of personalities, tastes, and interests to make the results worthy of the effort.

WHEN WIVES ATTEND

President Nixon's move to encourage Cabinet wives to attend periodic briefings so that they "will give them a sense of participation and will keep them informed of what their husbands are doing" has given executive wives a new pitch for togetherness.

Opinions differ on whether wives are an asset or a liability in business entertaining. However, the present trend is definitely in favor of including them whenever possible. Whether she plays an active role in her husband's business or a passive one, the wife is likely to accompany him on some of his business trips, or cohost with him when he is entertaining out-of-town clients or associates.

A LITTLE CONSIDERATION
GOES A LONG WAY

Small courtesies and thoughtfulness add up to grateful appreciation. Sometimes checking the accommodations at the hotel or motel might be necessary for the comfort of the guests. Alerting the hotel staff that the visitors are guests of the corporation will encourage them to extend themselves.

One top-management official in a real-estate syndicate, which was recently involved in some spectacular mergers requiring numerous executive conferences in various cities, had a foolproof way of charming accompanying wives. His secretary arranged to have flowers sent to greet their arrival at the hotel. Instructions were underlined to the florists that only arrangements in attractive containers should be sent, thereby saving the guests from the nuisance of having to scout around for vases for cut flowers. When the stay was expected to be more than a two-day session, his secretary made sure that a basket of fruit was sent, a courtly gesture that enchanted the ladies and gratified the husbands.

NEWSWORTHY EXECUTIVES

If the visiting executive is a person of particular importance, or has news value, check with your public-relations department and evaluate whether the press should be informed or a release be prepared.

Expressions of little niceties are always good, especially if they include the wives. This is when the resident executive wife can take over.

HELPFUL HINTS TO RESIDENT WIVES

(1) When the guests arrive at their hotel, some resident wives telephone the women guests for a get-acquainted chat.

(2) The resident wife might live in the suburbs and have a baby-sitter problem. Much as she would like to make herself available to show the visitor around, it may not always be possible.

One resident wife solved the problem by the simple expedient of preparing a list of important or amusing events scheduled in the city during the visitor's stay. While chatting she attempted to find out the guest's interests and clued her in accordingly. She included in her list art exhibits, concerts, the best places to browse for antiques, auction sales, the stores that have model-room exhibits, as well as stores where name-designer clothes are available and the little boutiques with their large stock of the unusual and hard-to-find accessories and gifts.

(3) During the telephone girl-talk the women exchange views on what to wear for dinner that evening, so that neither one is embarrassed by under- or over-dressing.

(4) Though etiquette requires the woman to extend the invitation to dinner, quasi-business-social dinners, including the evening entertainment, are frequently arranged by the men. Women have to accept their status as second in command. They cannot run the show as they might at home.

(5) Whatever her opinion of her husband's business guests,

the wife should present her most gracious and receptive façade.

(6) During such a semi-business-social occasion, a wife's attitude toward her husband is of utmost importance. An intelligent, sensitive woman can convey, without being too obvious about it, her esteem for her husband's professional status and achievements. This may prove a personality bonus to which any business guest will respond.

THE RESTAURANT SCENE

If there are more than two couples, the host, rather than the hostess, will suggest the seating arrangement—another departure from the accepted social procedure. The hostess defers to the guests and waits until each of the women is seated before she takes her place.

Business is hardly ever discussed at such dinner parties, though in-jokes and anecdotes do come up. It is inadvisable for the wives to enter into the discussion if a business subject is brought up. This occasion is *strictly* for men only. Even if the wife knows something the men are not aware of, she does her husband a great favor by keeping silent.

Unlike a social event when you can select your guests, in a business situation persons are thrown together whether they like one another or not. An executive has to have the tact of a diplomat and the savoir faire of a sophisticate to juggle an evening with assorted couples, some of whom may be not only total strangers but potentially antagonistic types. He has to keep a steely eye out to make sure that the wine glasses are kept filled, but not when one or more of the guests displayes obvious signs that the grape is taking over. He has to devise a discreet sign to the waiter that the wine ceremony is finished.

An overindulged guest or his wife who behaves with a lack of restraint or decorum will react with shame and embarrassment the next day and will doubtless harbor resentment against the host executive.

If for some reason you have a complaint about the service, call the waiter or the captain over and tell him in a low voice what you want done. The restaurant is no place to exhibit your executive authority.

THE EXPENSE-ACCOUNT GAMBIT

The swindle sheet is an old joke, and it is about time to put it back into mothballs. It is absurd, undignified, and, needless to say, dishonest, for a young executive to waste perfectly good brain energy trying to figure out petty thievery angles when submitting his out-of-pocket expenses and his credit-card charges.

A common caper is to take a friend out to lunch. You ask him: "Would you like to buy a hundred tons of slightly used electronic equipment?" He will answer: "No, not today, thanks." You then say: "I didn't think you would. But now I can justify our lunch as a business expense."

Comptrollers are notably humorless where corporate finances are concerned. Don't put yourself in the spot where your expense account becomes the object of the comptroller's careful scrutiny.

12. The Club in Town

Membership in a prestigious club in town, whether social, professional, university, or athletic, is not only a status-plus for a young executive but also a convenience: a *pied-à-terre* to entertain business associates, or arrange an overnight stay for an out-of-town visitor.

ARE YOU ELIGIBLE?

The first question you should ask yourself is whether you are eligible. Membership in some clubs, particularly athletic, is merely a matter of filling out a form and paying the dues.

But many clubs have membership requirements and pride themselves on their exclusivity. Openly applying to the secretary or the admissions committee for membership in such a club is breaking the ground rules. One must be "invited," that is, sponsored by a member in good standing and seconded by one or two other members.

Jerome Beatty, Jr., tells a story about the famous journalist, Richard Harding Davis, who had heard so much about the Farragut Club from Oliver Herford that he asked the poet to propose him for membership. After months of impatient waiting, Davis, who had been received graciously by heads of state in every part of the world, was outraged to be told by Herford that his membership application had been rejected. Ultimately, it was discovered that Herford was the club's sole member, that he held all the offices, and that the meetingplace was the bench under the statue of Admiral Farragut in Madison Square. Herford had organized the club for the sole purpose of blackballing Richard Harding Davis!

You have to be just as selective about the person who is sponsoring you as you are about the choice of club to which you wish to belong. Your sponsor-friend may be a regular fellow on the surface, but if he has any odd personality quirks, don't let him be the person to recommend you. He may not be popular among his fellow members, and they would not react too kindly to any proposal from him. Being rejected by a club is not only embarrassing but can prove to be somewhat traumatic.

If you do make the first move to join a club, the only logical person for you to approach to sponsor you for membership is a good friend, someone you are sure has your interest at heart. Don't ask or expect a person who does not know you well to be your sponsor. Even if he is too polite to turn you down, outright, he will mark you as a "pushy fellow" and not a suitable clubmate.

Before a young executive is carried away by his ambition to join a club, he should familiarize himself with its bylaws, as well as its rules and regulations, to be certain that he is eligible in every way, and that this is his kind of club.

DUES

Initiation fees and annual dues may run high in some of the clubs. Good judgment dictates that an aspirant should find this out before he has to hock his soul to keep up the payments.

Some companies recognize the value of membership in certain clubs, and they pay the initiation fees as well as the annual dues for those executives whose business activities overflow into social responsibilities. This is *sub rosa,* and by no means an open policy. It is done only for a select few; so before you have high hopes about boarding the gravy train, make discreet inquiries. Your superior and personnel director are the only ones who can guide you on the policy of the company in this regard.

One of your associates may tell you that his club membership is being underwritten by the company, or you may learn about it through some whispered confidence. You cannot take it for granted that your dues will be paid as well. There may be a good underlying reason why the company considers it desirable to have some members of the management belong to certain clubs.

CLUB ETIQUETTE

Many executives regard their private club as a safety hatch where they can find some peace, quiet, and relaxation. New members do not approach other members and open a conversation. They wait until the club manager or a mutual friend has introduced them properly. Occasionally an habitual member will notice a new face, speak to the freshman member, and perhaps introduce him to some of his cronies.

Some club dining rooms have one large "social" table for members who are lunching or dining alone. Here the conversation is general, and a new member is likely to meet and get to know the other members.

Facilities

Club facilities should be respected. Many club secretaries have to maintain a "Craig's Wife" attitude toward housekeeping, and careless habits may give the house committee cause to be churlish. The club's bylaws and the rules and regulations are required reading for every new member. He might have certain casual habits his indulgent wife overlooks, such as leaving smoldering cigars, pipes, or cigarettes in ashtrays, or scattering newspapers, magazines, or books and not returning them to their proper racks. These and other such acts of negligence are not trivial; older members are apt to be cantankerous about such matters and may mark them as misdemeanors.

A new member might also try to subdue his impulses and curb his exuberance until he gets to know the habitués. Some members may not be inclined to make new friends. There are men who go to their clubs in order to relax and get away from it all.

Guests

Guest privileges are extended by many clubs to out-of-town visitors for varying lengths of time. The courteous procedure is for the host member to accompany the guest to the club, introduce him to the secretary or the manager, and obtain a guest card for him.

It is assumed that a member will use his discretion in extending such privilege to a guest whose demeanor and general behavior will not be a discredit to him. Some bylaws permit only a limited number of guests for each member, so the better part of wisdom is for the host to be selective.

No guest should take the liberty of criticizing the service, the food, or the facilities of the club, any more than he would tell his host at a private dinner party that the food is not up to standard.

A guest in a club should be agreeable but unobtrusive, and make no unnecessary demands on the club employees.

The Club Chits

Very seldom does one pay in cash for drinks, food, or other services in American clubs. If the guest's card entitles him to "service privileges" then he signs his own name to each check.

The policy about tipping varies; some clubs include service charges in the bill, others leave it to the discretion of the patron. The discernment that stops short of overtipping without slipping into the pique-provoking error of undertipping is a talent worth cultivating. It is part of the sophisticated executive's survival equipment.

If the visitor is staying at the club as a guest of the corporation, he need not, of course, concern himself with the bill. But if he is being accommodated by a friendly associate and the club does not accept nonmember checks, the guest would wish to take care of the financial details without delay. He might enclose his check with his letter of thanks.

When he reimburses his host, the guest should also remember to check the club telephone operator for the local and long-distance calls he has made, as well as any other expenses he might have incurred.

In some clubs only chits signed by members are acceptable. In that case, the guest signs his host's name but adds his own name or his initials so that the records can be kept straight.

13. The Suburbia-Exurbia Exodus

The exodus of industries to surburbia to escape high realty rates and high city taxes is now spreading out into exurbia. Gleaming steel and dazzling glass buildings disguising factories, mills, and administration offices are mushrooming in wooded areas throughout the country. Industry and therefore executives have to learn to coexist with nature, where the social action is practically intramural.

While these company "towns" are proliferating in the name of economic progress, an introverted social order is imposed upon the employees. They are bound together in their daily business life, and out of sheer necessity and isolation they are thrown together willy-nilly into a social mélange. Not all executives and their wives have the same cultural or regional background, but they all have the same human urge for companionship and the need to communicate. Their physical isolation leaves them only their own resources for intellectual and spiritual nourishment. Little-theater groups are formed, and jazz combos find that their associates and friends are their most enthusiastic audiences.

Because of the insular character of these "business-industrial islands," visitors of whatever level become somewhat of a problem. Home entertainment is not always welcomed by a busy wife and mother, while the restaurants often leave a great deal to be desired. Hence, the average executive is up against it.

Unless the company has its own dining facilities where visitors can be entertained, it often means going quite a distance to find a restaurant with good food and a pleasant decor.

THE WAY TO A WOMAN'S HEART

A synthetic fiber division of a multimillion-dollar corporation is located in North Carolina, twelve miles from the nearest town. There is no dining room, not even an employees' cafeteria, in any of the several buildings dotting the landscape. The personnel, including the executives, have any of the following choices:

(1) Avail themselves of the chuck wagon with its mediocre sandwiches, soggy pies, and coffee in paper cups.

(2) Bring their own lunches, which the executives eat at their desks.

(3) Rush home to their split-levels, if time permits, and gulp down a hot meal; that is, if their wives are at home and have the time to prepare it.

(4) Drive twelve miles to the nearest decent restaurant.

Three women executives from the company's New York office—the publicity director and the coordinators of fashions and home furnishings—were sent to this plant for a two-day indoctrination.

Professionally, the women had no complaints. They were shown what they had to see and what they wanted to know. At noon they were in the conference room taking copious notes and directives from the manager of the dye-processing plant. The general manager's secretary interrupted to ask what they would like for lunch, adding that the chuck wagon was now open.

During the process of deciding between a ham on rye and a cheese sandwich, the manager excused himself and left. When the secretary returned with the paper bags of sandwiches and coffee, she informed each of the women executives: "You owe 65¢; you owe 80¢;" and one was $1.05 because an order of fruit salad was included.

The luncheon was a hilarious session for the women who couldn't quite decide how they would show these figures on their expense accounts.

At closing time, when the last car drove out of the executive parking lot, the women found themselves on their own. One of the executives did tell them about a fairly good restaurant, if they felt like driving to town.

The women spent their evening in a serious discussion. Each of the executives whom they met that day must have had an extensive educational background to qualify for the job he had to perform. The men seemed outwardly polite, professionally cooperative, and some even volunteered information about themselves: their life in a company-oriented community, the little-theater group they and their wives had formed; the folk-singing group that was invited to perform in the community hall and the parish church. But they failed in one essential quality—humane consideration and concern for visitors in a strange community.

One of the women excused the men: "They were probably too busy and preoccupied with their responsibilities." But the other two women insisted that *thoughtlessness is discourtesy,* and that discourtesy in any form is inexcusable.

The plane trip home provided a strategy session for the three disenchanted women. Should they present the matter before a policy meeting? Or should they take it upon themselves to demonstrate the true meaning of hospitality? They agreed on the latter.

Some days later, they learned that the general manager and a supervisor would be arriving in New York. A teletype was dispatched asking if the men would be free for dinner the day of their arrival. The teletyped response could be interpreted only by a psychologist for its overtones of executive insecurity: "Yes, but what's up?"

The women started the evening with drinks in the publicity director's home. In a relaxed atmosphere, fortified by cocktails and hors d'oeuvres, the men soon shed their uptight executive controls and turned into agreeable, appreciative guests.

Dinner was at a restaurant with a reputation for good food and attractive surroundings. Nothing was mentioned about the visit the women had made to their plant, but the general manager had the grace to say: "I don't know how to thank you for this wonderful evening, except to ask that you come back to visit us, so that we can show you that we too can be hospitable."

This incident resulted in some interesting "humanizing" side effects. Thereafter, whenever any of the New York executives visited the plant, they no longer spent lonely evenings watching TV in their motel rooms. Instead, they were invited to the homes of the resident executives, where they enjoyed barbecued dinners, pleasant social interchange, and a release from business tensions.

The reciprocal hospitality did more than merely provide a climate of friendly rapport. The business relationship between the executives became more flexible, and their channels of communication more fluid, thus eliminating considerable wear and tear of executive nerves. This not only benefitted the executives but in the long run showed up in black on the balance sheet.

DINNER IN THE BOSS'S HOME

Not infrequently, a young executive and his wife are invited to the boss's home for dinner. This is likely to occur in the suburban areas more often than in the city.

While the boss may suggest the idea to the young executive, it is usually the hostess who extends the invitation to the wife.

The first visit to the boss's home is in a sense a command performance. You and your wife should work out a strategy plan.

(1) For better rapport, try to find out what the boss's wife's interests and hobbies are. It is possible that his secretary knows. Inform your wife so that she can do her homework. In the rural areas it is quite likely that the women attend the same flower-arranging classes, or they may have met at the country club. But if the young couple are new arrivals in the community, it is best to be forewarned and forearmed.

(2) Your wife may have a mink coat which she dearly loves, but persuade her not to wear it on her first visit to your boss's home. If his wife doesn't own a mink coat, this may become a "memorable" evening for your boss!

(3) The same applies to an excess of jewelry and her mini-skirted dress. She may look ravishing in her new satin pants suit designed just for evening wear, but she will only expose herself as knowing style but not good taste. A simple, conventional frock is her best choice.

(4) Your boss may be the slacks-and-sport-jacket type. Unless he suggests otherwise, you as a guest in his home should wear a conservative business suit, white or light colored shirt, and a subdued tie.

(5) If you address your boss as "Mr." in the office, continue to do so in his home, even though his wife refers to him as "John." Only when he suggests it himself should you call him by his Christian name.

A famous publisher invited some of the members of his editorial staff to his home for Sunday brunch. One young man interpreted this to mean that he was now regarded as a friend as well as an employee. Right there and then he addressed his boss by his first name and continued to do so throughout the afternoon. He was fired the very next month.

(6) Similarly, you should address your hostess as "Mrs." unless she suggests that you do otherwise.

(7) When you are speaking of your wife, you refer to her as "Mary" or "my wife." You use the prefix "Mrs." only when you are talking about her to strangers who are not in your social circle, to servants, and to children.

(8) When it comes to predinner drinks, both you and your wife would be wise to limit yourselves to no more than two drinks. Any more might be an invitation to trouble. If wine is served, it is advisable to sip slowly and not to encourage refills.

(9) Do not discuss business unless your boss introduces the subject, which is doubtful. If business is discussed, your wife must stay out of it even if the boss's wife feels she must have her say.

(10) Do not overstay your welcome. A show of good manners is not only following the rules of etiquette but the instinct to understand and comply with the other person's needs. A long-drawn-out evening may turn a pleasant social occasion into a tiring bore. Ten o'clock is a reasonable hour to begin showing signs that you are ready to leave unless your boss is in the midst of telling you how he had made that touchdown for his college team, or his wife is telling your wife how to keep a cheese soufflé from flopping. Most young couples have a built-in valid excuse. They have to drive the baby-sitter home.

THE BREAD-AND-BUTTER LETTER

Just as bread is verboten in some diets and margarine is substituted for butter, so the customary thank-you note that dinner guests used to send to the hostess has fallen victim to er-satz-courtesy. Nowadays, most guests, as they are departing, tell the host and hostess how much they enjoyed the dinner, thank them for an enjoyable evening, and let it go at that. Sometimes a woman guest will telephone the hostess the next day, but this is more in the nature of a postprandial exchange of recipes and gossip, with a few kind words about the evening incidentally thrown in.

An interesting reference is made in *Hints on Etiquette,* written in 1834 and reproduced by E. P. Dutton & Co. in 1951: "It is customary, when you have been out dining, to leave a card upon the lady next day, or as soon as may be convenient.

"Attentions of this sort are not to be expected from professional men, as Doctors, Lawyers, etc., *their* time being too valuable to sacrifice in making visits of mere ceremony; therefore, do not attribute such omission to any want of respect, but to its proper cause—*time more usefully occupied.*"

Yet, today there are certain occasions when a thank-you letter is the courteous thing to do!

When a couple are guests at a dinner party arranged in their honor to meet associates or other guests, a note of appreciation expressing thanks is sure to have a favorable reaction.

For an overnight or weekend stay, a bread-and-butter letter is almost mandatory.

Flowers accompanying a thank-you note will enhance your words and charm your hostess.

HAVING YOUR BOSS FOR DINNER

You and your wife will want to return the courtesy and invite your boss and his wife to your home for dinner. It is assumed that you would not presume to invite them if they had not made the first move.

Once again it is the hostess who extends the invitation. However, if there are any doubts in your mind about the advisability of such a move, you might mention casually to your boss that your wife will be in touch with his wife about a dinner date and you trust that it is okay with him.

Don't invite any other guests if your boss and his wife are

expected to dine with you. Not even your rich uncle from Kalamazoo or your best friend whose father is the president of a bank. Personality clashes are risky enough in a social environment; in a business situation they are disastrous.

Don't attempt to show off to your boss and his wife by having an elaborate dinner with fancy trimmings.

One young couple did, even to the extent of renting a silver coffee and tea service. The children were sent off to bed early and warned not to make any disturbance. The host's and the hostess's nervous concern that everything had to be just right charged the air. The dinner was stiff and formal. The hostess was on edge and the guests couldn't help being aware of it. The host tried to be jocular but his efforts met with feeble response. Finally, the dinner was over and the hostess suggested that they retire to the living room for coffee. The young woman poured from the silver coffee urn and her husband did the cream and sugar bit. It was just then that the patter of little feet was heard. The pajama-clad figure of their little girl appeared. In a small voice she asked: "Please, Daddy, can I see what your Mr. Whizbang boss looks like?"

Never had the young man heard his boss laugh so heartily. It broke the tension, and the evening was saved.

You may be a hi-fi buff, but before you attempt to entertain your boss and his wife with your selections, better find out if they like music.

In rural areas, company life too often impinges on social life and conflicting cultures may stir up curious reactions.

Frank S. was transferred from the New York office to the company plant in upper Westchester. His supervisor and his wife took a paternal interest in Frank and his young family—until the older couple visited the younger couple in their new home.

At eight o'clock the boss asked Frank, "Where's your TV? I don't want to miss 'All in the Family.' " Instead of answering politely that they did not own a TV set, the young man's intellectual arrogance got the better of his judgment and he replied: "We don't want to expose our children to the junk shown on TV—not yet anyhow—so we won't have a set in our home."

At first the boss thought Frank was putting him on; but when he realized that he was serious, the older man felt not only snubbed but that his way of life had been rejected as un-worthy.

The older couple left early, and the paternal interest in Frank and his career faded.

Your wife and you like to dress informally when you are at home. But when you entertain, a courteous compliment to your guests is to dress *appropriately* for the occasion.

Your boss and his wife are not run-of-the-mill guests. Your off-the-job relationship with him may prove as decisive as your working association in the office.

If your superior is the type who is generally resistant to change, the fact that Lord Snowdon prefers turtleneck sweaters wouldn't register with him. Nor would he and his wife react with favor if your wife took the fashion maga-zines' dictum literally that this is "the year of the anatomy." She would shock them if she welcomed them wearing the far-out fun clothes that feature the nude-midriff look.

But the wave of the future is now becoming a tidal storm washing away many old conventions and traditions. You and your wife believe in doing your own thing. You are deter-mined not to allow yourself to be shaped into an "organization man." You will not permit management to make you con-form to the corporate concept of the stereotyped executive. In your own home at least, you are master of your own soul.

Very well. You wear what you feel most comfortable in, but with sufficient restraint so that you do not flabbergast or shock your guests whose standards and tastes you would do well to respect.

For the Man of the House

If being encased in a jacket with your neck constricted by a carefully knotted tie makes no sense to you when you are in your own home, then wear a sport shirt and slacks. But show that you care by adding one of those printed silk scarves that are worn loosely knotted around the neck. They have style and put the finishing touch to the most casual costume.

If you are not secure unless you wear your turtleneck sweater, just be sure you keep the beads and the medallions in the drawer. One ad manager's flippant good night to his associates ended in a good-bye when he loudly proclaimed as he left the office: "Now I can go home and change my tie for my beads." His associates thought it was funny, but management read a deeper meaning into it.

For the Lady of the House

The bare midriff won't do; neither will the neckline that doesn't stop plunging until it reaches the waist; the mod cutouts revealing tantalizing parts of the body will alienate rather than please; and bare legs in thonged sandals will indicate that you are just a little too casual.

Pants suits are in and a blessing in a servantless household where the wife has to be cook, waitress, and a charming hostess rolled into one.

If you are the least doubtful, your self-esteem and individuality will not suffer if you choose the safest course—a simple frock for the hostess and the traditional business suit for the host.

A NOT-SO-GENTLE REMINDER

In company towns, the business and social life are almost synonymous, providing a hospitable climate for warm human relationships. But it is also a hazardous environment that calls for a cool head to maintain the working posture without the infringement of personal sentiments or attachments.

Intimate friendships with your boss and any other associates can spell job disaster. One minor quarrel, one social misstep, and your working defenses—impartial judgment, orderly procedure, and objectivity—collapse into a hostile crisis.

You would do well to caution your wife not to become too intimate with the other executives' wives. Exchange of confidences can bring on personal revelations that have no part in the business world, which has its own quota of gossip and scuttlebutt to combat.

14. The Country Club

MEMBERSHIP

At one time young executives joined clubs for status, and to exploit potential business contacts among well-heeled habitués, as well as for front-office entertaining.

Today, they are more realistic and frankly admit that the country club is their escape hatch. The average executive leads a sedentary life. Physical fitness is a slogan he is too busy to put into daily action. However, the country club offers him and every member of his family sports facilities, including supervised activities for the small-fry.

Some hinterland country clubs are family-oriented and informal. Generally an application to the club secretary is all that is required. There are, of course, the exclusive country clubs with limited membership and implicit standards, where one doesn't ask to join but must wait to be invited. The procedure is the same as in town clubs. You are proposed by one member and sponsored by one or two other members.

If you are a newcomer to the community, a hint to a friendly neighbor might get you the necessary introductions to one or two members to qualify you for admission to the local club.

After your name and your sponsors' names are posted, some of the clubs will notify their entire membership by letter outlining your essential qualifications. You and your wife will probably be required to meet with the admissions committee for a personal interview to determine whether you both pass muster, and your references are carefully checked.

If this gamut is not enough, some clubs have a sixty-day trial membership. People-watchers are all over the place, and if you or your wife is found wanting in the social graces, you may expect a letter of regret rather than a confirmation of your membership.

One commuting executive has decided that his country club is his second home after computing the number of hours he spends there for sports, recreation, relaxation, and congenial companionship. He has no compunctions about reporting social blunders to the grievance committee, especially when such blunders are objectionable and interfere with the concept of club decorum, or violate any of the rules and regulations. A member was asked to resign because he was overbearing and dictatorial in his treatment of the club staff; another found himself to be an unwanted member when he strenuously argued with the golf pro about replacing divots he had hacked away on the green. A club on Long Island asked a member to resign when his wife neglected to ration her drinks at the bar and made an unpleasant spectacle of herself.

RULES AND REGULATIONS

In addition to the bylaws, all clubs have two sets of rules.

(1) The written rules and regulations that spell out the club's character and the expected behavior of each member.

(2) The unwritten rules, which are implicit, and just as important, and in which the individual's behavior, in Goethe's words, is reflected as in "a mirror in which everyone shows his image."

The club is a homogeneous society where each person is charged with strict adherence to the written rules and the intuitive observance of the unwritten ones. No one can barge in and take over; nor can the club be used as a stage for any anti-hero antics.

There are no points in etiquette that can or should be dismissed as trivial. One may observe the bylaws meticulously, and then commit an inexcusable, thoughtless act, such as arriving at the club during a weekend with a horde of guests. Weekends are when members like to enjoy the club facilities.

It is indefensible and bad form for you and your guests to occupy the tennis, badminton, or squash courts to the exclusion of members. If you suspect that any of your guests are golfduffers, try to persuade them to go swimming instead. Members who are held up on the golf course, especially by outsiders, are not apt to be kindly disposed to their member host.

If your friends are apt to be boisterous drinkers, your armor for self-preservation should encourage you to entertain them in your home, rather than at the club.

DUES AND CLUB BILLS

Don't allow your dues to accumulate and your bills to run over one "balance due." Being posted for nonpayment is not only damaging to your social reputation but it is sure to tarnish your executive standing.

GUEST PRIVILEGES FOR BUSINESS ASSOCIATES

Business entertaining at a country club changes "duty" and "chore" into a do-it-yourself snap. Temporary membership or guest privilege cards can be obtained in many clubs. This is a special advantage when a business associate's stay is prolonged for several days or over a weekend. It is not always necessary for the member-host to accompany the guest and introduce him. In the main, country clubs are informal, and it is not unusual for a stranger to be invited to make up a foursome for a golf game or a tennis match. In fact, some clubs have a ruling that a twosome has no standing on weekends and holidays if there are other players available.

Many clubs designate a house guest as "anyone residing one hundred or more miles away."

No cash is used in country-club transactions. Chits are signed, either with the member-host's name, initialed by the guest, or the guest's own name, according to prior arrangements. In all clubs a service charge is included in the bill.

15. Anchors Aweigh

When 3.15 billion dollars are spent in a single year for the purchase of pleasure boats, which include everything from cruisers, sailboats, houseboats, and runabouts to jet boats, it cannot be regarded as a fad but a burgeoning trend. It is estimated that the national flotilla currently numbers about 8.5 million boats exploring America's waterways.

A dry-docked executive will find himself in the minority, and if he wants to be in the swim, he may have to hock his swimming pool, which is fast becoming a quaint memento of his past.

SAILING P'S AND Q'S

Seafaring etiquette is of necessity strict. Safety is the number-one consideration, though there are other procedures a landlubber cannot and must not ignore.

(1) Never accept an invitation on any type of boat, no matter how small or large, if you turn green at the sight of water. Mal de mer is unpleasant not only for the sufferer but for the other members of the party.

(2) On yachts or mini-yachts where there are a captain and a crew, the captain is in command. Everyone, including the owner, defers to the captain's orders. He is called either "Captain," "Mr.," or by his surname. The paid hands are also called by their last names.

(3) If the boat is a crewless one, prepare yourself to lend

a hand: hoisting or lowering of sails, pumping out the bilge. At all times be ready to obey the commands of your host, who is captain of the ship, and whose orders are inviolable.

(4) Keep your luggage to a minimum—one bag only. There is no room for heavy or stiff luggage. Use a canvas duffel bag or anything collapsible that can be easily stowed.

(5) If you are in doubt about clothing, consult your host or hostess, and save yourself from being a nuisance by having to borrow something you need. Denims, sweaters, wool socks, a waterproof coat or jacket, swimsuit, and perhaps shorts will suffice for a short cruise. Don't forget your dark glasses and a headcover—the sun might be broiling or the wind turn frisky. You must have rubber-soled shoes to wear on the boat. Hardsoled shoes or high heels are definitely out. You'll need a going-on-shore jacket, which you can tuck away in the locker until you need it.

(6) Don't dive overboard for a swim without your host's permission and instructions from where it would be safe to take the plunge. If the boat is in motion, a towline is necessary.

(7) Smoking on some boats is a safety hazard. If your host-captain permits it, be sure to toss your lighted cigarette or cigar overboard to leeward; otherwise the wind may return the sparks right back. If you are uncertain which is leeward and which is windward, use an ashtray. Never throw your cigarette on deck and stamp it out.

(8) Garbage or other refuse should not be thrown overboard, especially when the boat is in harbor or moored in a marina or a yacht basin. Boat owners keep a supply of disposable bags for garbage and trash.

(9) The galley is off limits to guests unless invited and well briefed about the workings of all the gadgets and other intricacies.

GIFT-BEARING GUESTS

Boat owners have to run a tight ship. There is no room for clutter or unnecessary articles. A guest who wishes to bring a gift, or make some contribution to the galley, would be wise to consult his host or hostess first; otherwise his offering might turn out to be just so much flotsam and jetsam.

Most individuals adore getting gifts, even when they mumble, "You shouldn't have done it," or words to that effect. There is an art in giving as well as in receiving. A friendly, frank exchange of ideas will take the "what-to-bring" out of the nitty-gritty and turn it into something meaningful and pleasurable.

Some guests prefer to wait until after the visit to send their tokens of appreciation. Then they are better aware of what is needed and can be used.

Whether you send a gift-wrapped package or not, when Blue Monday comes around and you are back at the old grind, take time out to write a thank-you note. It is a nice warm greeting to the boat owner and his wife when they anchor in port.

16. The Company Plane

FLYING HIGH

The significance of the corporate jet in industry is that it has encouraged business to expand its horizons and facilitate decentralization programs. Top management can now supervise operations at subsidiaries in different locations without having to stay away from their home bases for any extended length of time.

The National Business Aircraft Association defines "corporate (executive) aircraft" as any plane operated by a full-time professionally qualified pilot.

The corporate jet, or as it is more frequently referred to, the company plane, usually takes on the characteristics of its corporate ownership, and like a home, it reflects the personalities of the people who live in it or use it. If management is rigid, the executive plane is exclusively the province of the top group and is used solely for their transportation and, of course, that of any of their guests who most likely are of equal stature.

Those companies that have a no-alcoholic-beverages-on-the-premises policy observe the same rules on their planes. Travelers have to be content to fly high on soft drinks.

When it comes to the company plane, the young executive is the low man on the totem pole. In some corporations he has to wait until a ranking executive invites him, or makes the necessary arrangements for him to use the plane when he is scheduled for a business trip.

Other companies are more flexible. They treat their executive planes for what they are—a speedy transport convenience for the company personnel. Legitimate business errands, no matter who carries the attaché case, get priority. High-altitude snobbism does not exist, and no one is treated as a hitchhiker, not even the freshman executive. Once he is on the plane, he is in.

There are also companies where top management likes to keep their public image polished to a shiny glow. Their planes are apt to have at least two stewards, or stewardesses, who are obviously charter members of the Society for the Prevention of Cruelty to Executives. Drinks, alcoholic and otherwise, are readily available and the galley is well stocked with food.

Many of the planes are convertible into airborne offices. They are designed for comfort as well as for work. One section of the cabin may be handsomely appointed with a table and seats to accommodate a small conference or meeting. Another section has regulation airplane seats, where the young executive may sit quietly by himself contemplating "the infinite meadows of heaven." But in many cases, these seats are adjustable and can be set up in different ways so that two or three executives can have a quick meeting or a private brainstorming session of their own.

The latest innovation is the new flying jet palace, costing between three and four million dollars, which can only be described as a luxurious auxiliary company office and conference quarters. This new type of business aircraft is self-contained and self-sufficient. It is capable of making nonstop flights across the continent or across the ocean. It can carry more than 100 passengers, as well as cargo. Another long-range company jet can carry as many as 189 passengers; it has sleeping compartments and a galley, of course.

Its true *raison d'être*, however, is its commodious cabin outfitted and equipped for any type of meeting or a sales demonstration. For the time being, or at least until such business jets become the norm, executives charged with the duty of organizing meetings or sales pitches need not go into a tailspin. Customers or distributors, however recalcitrant, will not be able to resist an invitation for a pie-in-the-sky hoopla. Customers will be sold by the time they set foot on the gangplank because human nature being what it is, vanity conquers judgment.

These business-oriented jets can land at any airport, or even in certain areas that are not commerically serviced. They could be grounded in the vicinity of the company's branch offices, factories, warehouses, or other holdings, and on-the-spot meetings or conferences could be held there and then.

On a junket of this type, a young executive is thrust into a dual role. On the plane, among his superiors and peers, he conforms to normal office procedure. He stays in the background and only projects himself when his services are needed. When there are guests, whether they are customers, suppliers, or resident executives, however, he may offer his help to the ranking executive and assume the role of an assistant host. Without being too persistent, he may see to it that a guest's glass is refilled, or inquire whether he wants another portion of the chef's *spécialité du jour*, and in general try to be of assistance. It is assumed that a man of any sensitivity will recognize when his attentions are becoming troublesome, and he will know when to desist.

A FEW DON'TS

Whether the company plane is one of those new glamorous super jetliners, merely a modest quarter-of-a-million-dollar job, or simply a mundane six-seater, the same etiquette that represents top management's posture prevails.

There are certain subtle nuances applicable to company-plane etiquette, about which a grounded executive might be forewarned and hence forearmed:

(1) Every executive should ask himself if the trip is necessary before he signs up for a jaunt. He is not getting a free ride. Business operates on the theory that anything anyone gets for nothing he values at nothing. Costs for the use of the company plane are charged to the executive's department, usually prorated on the same basis that regular commercial airlines charge. An excessive amount of charges for the use of the company plane by one individual may invite a showdown with the higher in command. Or just as likely, the comptroller may want to ask a few questions, and everybody knows how befogged a comptroller's visibility can be by facts and figures. An enthusiastic plane-hopping executive had bet-

ter be in a solid position of being able to justify each trip
with a good business reason.

(2) The worst blunder, both businesswise and socially, is
to be responsible in any way for delaying the departure of
the executive plane. Some companies provide door-to-airport
limousine service. But whatever the facilities, no executive
can afford the onus of throwing a monkey wrench into the
works. At the rendezvous point, the executive should be
ahead of time. Nothing can tarnish a young hopeful's image
more than to keep his superiors fidgeting, waiting for the
takeoff, because of his delinquency. Nor is he exactly a pre-
possessing spectacle when he is seen racing along the runway,
losing his dignity and showing his guilt on the way to the
boarding ramp.

(3) Personal baggage should be kept to a minimum, particularly on convention or sales-promotion trips, when the
cargo section is probably loaded to capacity with all the
necessary sales, advertising, publicity, and promotional material. Small bags can be placed on the baggage rack, but never
heavy or cumbersome pieces. The most suitable airplane luggage, of course, is the lightweight, canvas type that can be
easily stowed.

(4) The pilot is the captain, and his decisions must be respected and followed. The pilot has to comply with all the
federal and state aviation rules and follow tower instructions.
It is up to him to gauge when and if he can take off and
where and when he makes an emergency landing. In addition, his own experience and his expertise dictate when he
thinks it is advisable for the plane to be airborne, when passengers must not smoke, or when they should fasten their
seat belts. Not even the chairman of the board or the president of the company can contradict or impose any changes
in the pilot's orders.

(5) The president of the company may call the steward or
the stewardess by the first name. This same privilege does not
necessarily extend to any other member of management. On
commercial flights one automatically says "stewardess." But
on a company plane the executive and the steward are presumably both members of one family. Usually the steward
greets guests and introduces himself when he boards the
plane. If he says his name is Dick, then that is how he wishes
to be addressed. But if he says his name is Dick Service, he is

Mr. Service unless he suggests otherwise. It is customary for the executive to give the steward his full name.

(6) Seating is generally informal, but no well-mannered, echelon-oriented executive would presume to seat himself next to the president if other high-ranking officials are on the plane. Middle-management and junior executives should casually linger in the background until top brass and other older executives have selected their seats.

(7) The cockpit is off limits for all passengers unless the pilot extends the invitation. This includes even those executives who are licensed and experienced pilots. They may itch to get their hands on the stick, but their services as copilot are not usually welcome. They are cast in the role of executive and they cannot always change uniforms in midair.

(8) Smoking on the company plane is one of those pesky "iffy" questions. Before anyone lights up, it is necessary to know the pilot's disposition on the subject. No smoking is permitted on commercial airliners before takeoff and landing. But every company has its own specific taboos dictated by the pilot, who may ban the use of lighters; or, as is the case in one company, a smoking taboo is dictated by the board chairman's allergy to tobacco smoke of any kind.

On a recent New York to Tulsa flight of a company's top management the wife of the president invited herself along. It was her husband's birthday, and she felt a celebration was due him. Her baggage included a case of champagne and other delicacies, as well as an enormous birthday cake with the proper number of candles. When the cake ceremony was ready to begin, the pilot came out and cautioned her that it was against the rules to light candles on the plane. Hence, the assembled guests had to have their fun huffing and puffing at the non-flickering tapers, singing their jolly good wishes.

(9) Shirt sleeves are accepted on company planes more so than in offices. It is not for us to reason why. It is just one of those anomalies where corporate dicta clash head-on with instinctive human reaction. As one executive explained: "I can't relax up there until I take off my jacket. Maybe I can even catch a snooze. But if any of the fellows wish to have a brain-picking session before we land, I have the feeling my sleeves are rolled up and I'm ready for action." Coats and jackets can be neatly folded and placed in the overhead racks, or given to the steward to hang up in the locker. They should not contribute to any clutter in the plane, nor should

they be hung where they would obstruct someone else's view.

(10) It is wise to refrain from jokes that refer to flight. These can easily antagonize the rest of the group. One young executive was very uncomfortable when he was treated as a pariah on the company plane. All he did, as he explained later, was to ask the pilot before takeoff to witness his last will and testament. The pilot was not amused, nor were his copassengers.

17. The Computer and You

The computer is Frankenstein's monster reincarnated. But instead of being evil, it is atoning for its past sins by reversing the old adage of "man's inhumanity to man." Today, it is the "machine's humanity to man."

This fast-thinking, fast-working analytical genius may not yet be capable of writing Shakespearean sonnets, but its prose is eloquently revealing, first probing into the very depths of your being and then coming up with words and figures of significance. It can virtually crawl into every pigeonhole of your brain and ferret out all the rights and wrongs—whether your department or division is up to standard, whether your company's profitability graph is on the rise or decline, and so on ad infinitum.

A child of the human brain, the computer is already surpassing its parent. And if the parent isn't on the alert, his creative robot may make a nonhero out of him. One mistake, one misstep, and the electronic wizard can be merciless. The machine makes no allowances for human frailties. Many an executive has lost his temper and accused the computer of being "a fink and a stool pigeon."

The computer, of course, takes no stock in any such outbursts. It hasn't yet mastered the ability to love or hate. Nor does it expect any love in return—not even tenderness. It refuses to recognize loyalty to anyone or anything except facts and figures. If it has a sense of humor, which is doubtful, it may laugh up its electronic sleeve when someone makes a mistake. Otherwise, it will just keep plodding along, rememering to break down every now and then, making sure that it is in the middle of a vitally important assignment.

Still, the computer has its own code of etiquette by continuing to do its work expertly, precisely, and thoroughly. It never gets tired and never complains. It is a well-mannered robot, and many an executive wishes some of his workers would be as uncomplaining and as productive.

The computer was actually invented in 1820 by an Englishman, Charles Babbage, who called it an "Analytical Engine." But the inventor and his robot were rejected as eccentric, and it wasn't until 1941 that a working computer made in Germany was recognized for its sophisticated limitless abilities.

It behooves each executive on the way up to learn to live with the computer, to learn its ways, its know-how, and the parameters of its capabilities, but, even more importantly, its specialized nomenclature. This is where your ignorance can make a dent in your executive armor. Today, the mental baggage of a well-bred executive must include the whole spectrum of the computer lingo.

COMPUTER DOUBLE-TALK

Electronic language has invaded our business world. It has a grammar and a syntax all its own. The executive who has only recently become acquainted with the computer might find himself at a loss. He may even feel embarrassed, because younger men of the corporation can toss off words he had never heard before. Don't let your status fray and be defeated by this.

If your corporation has not included you in the computer training session, get a glossary of computer terms from the company that installed it, or apply to the manufacturer for information. Read up on the subject. There is a plethora of material released not only in the trade and professional magazines but in the mass-circulation media, and there are many books published on the subject.

If, however, your computer expertise surpasses that of the others, don't be a computer "name-dropper." You may like to show off and toss your terminology around in front of the executives who are not too familiar with the lingo, but resist the temptation. Use your phraseology tactfully. Remember, boasting is not the quickest road to executive success, and it is questionable manners.

18. Industrial Recreational Programs

The quality of good sportsmanship is the basis of corporate etiquette—the key to whether you are an aggressive winner, a cooperative team member, or a disgruntled loser.

The burgeoning industrial recreation programs encouraged and sponsored by management are testing grounds where one's agility of body and mind are equated with one's capacity to face up to competitive situations.

The company sports grounds, arenas, and gymnasiums offer congenial and fruitful environments to establish a camaraderie with all the members of the corporate family, from the front-office personnel to the blue-collar men, the overalled assemblyline workers, and the boys in the back room. One large company's bowling team, for example, includes the chairman of the board and the president. Basketball teams are also nonpartisan, and casualties occur without respect for rank or position. One corporation president had to be carried off the company court in the heat of the game with a torn Achilles' tendon. Nevertheless, he is continuing with plans to break ground for a new $750,000 seventy-acre recreation facility for his company. Similarly, the treasurer of a California company got somewhat chopped up in a karate bout with one of the production workers.

Parenthetically, it should be noted that physical fitness is a serious concern of corporate management. Executive physique, posture, and bearing are regarded as sufficiently important to list on the IBM classification sheet. In corporate parlance, a lean executive is healthy, alert, energetic, and his appearance does credit to the accepted executive image.

Currently, there are more than eight thousand companies that have full- or part-time recreation directors, while the majority of firms employing more than one thousand persons have initiated some form of athletic program.

Most companies have written rules with regard to locker rooms, sports equipment, and such. These usually follow the procedures of the average country club. No executive, of whatever echelon, would presume to take it upon himself to change or deviate from these rules. He will have to restrain his dictatorial impulses until such time as he himself becomes president, or at least executive vice-president.

But it is the area of the unwritten rules of corporate sportsmanship which marks the champion and separates him from the spoilsport.

(1) No executive can afford to remain exclusive or seclusive in any of the company recreational programs, which are geared to include every employee within the organization, as well as the families, and in some instances the rest of the community. Somewhere, somehow, the executive has to find his sports niche, and participate. The unathletic, disinclined executive, or one who is allergic to any kind of company togetherness, will have to begin to limber up his stagnant muscles. Today management's attitude is that industry's need is for individuals who are healthy, vigorous, and competitively keen.

(2) Teamwork is playing the game with grace, win or lose. The winning team may be jubilant, but never gloating or lording over the losing team. And no teammate should be singled out and rebuked for a misplay or an error. The captains of each team may exchange compliments: the winners for their skill, the losers for their good try.

(3) A new member joining a team may have to practice walking a tightrope—at first. He need not necessarily hover in the background, nor let his enthusiasm for a new sport carry him to extremes where he is likely to be classified as a boor. Middle-of-the-road conduct is best, letting the more experienced players lead the way.

(4) Each sport has its own set of rigid rules. However, some teams may relax or deviate from the accepted rules, which one should learn beforehand to qualify as a sportsman.

(5) There are occasions when being a good sport may require you to lose the game in order to prove it. When you are playing golf or tennis with your superior, or even with a

subordinate, and you excel at the game, give the other fellow a break. Let him win once in a while. Don't let him drag too many defeats away with him. A well-adjusted person is one who plays in any sport as if it were merely a game.

19. Business-Social Communications

EXPECTED AND UNEXPECTED EVENTS

A corporation is an assemblage of human beings from whom it derives its personality and traditions. It has a spirit of its own that needs some pampering and catering to, particularly in time of stress.

Even the mightiest corporations are not immune to suffering a sudden calamitous disaster. Airplane accidents have been known to deprive a single company of several important executives; fires and floods have brought about wholesale destruction of factories, equipment, valuable records, and just as often, personnel.

Then, of course, there are times when an organization experiences good fortune, such as the award of an astronomical government contract; the development of a record-breaking invention; the projection of the company into a major status in the corporate stratosphere as the result of a fortuitous acquisition; or relocation to new, grandiose offices. In addition, there is always the executive penchant for playing musical chairs: promotions within the company, the installation of new officials from other organizations, perhaps the departure of an executive for an important diplomatic post.

No executive, of whatever echelon, can afford to overlook or omit a courteous gesture of recognition when anything of significance happens. This applies not only to his own corporate family but to any organization with which he has had dealings. This is good manners and it also builds goodwill—a preface tō good business. The sales, advertising, publicity, and promotion program of a company must be supported by the individual conduct of an executive. An important part of the executive's job is to make friends for his company, and he can do so by exerting his personal effort and by demonstrating his interest and concern.

CONGRATULATORY MESSAGES

Who Talks to Whom?

"The Lowells speak only to Cabots and the Cabots speak only to God" is the undeclared corporate etiquette rule.

An executive addressing himself to someone in another company observes the code of procedure in respect to rank and position that prevails in his own organization. His message should be directed to the person with whom he has dealt, and who, most likely, is on the same level as he is. There are instances where he might also communicate with an executive who is a degree higher, or with a junior, who he knows is a white-haired hopeful on the way up. But he does not step too far out of the frame of his own rank. To do so would be a corporate blunder. He is likely to invite a shrug-off by the recipient who might feel that the message-sender is presumptuous and does not have company manners.

The same applies to his own organization. An executive must never lose sight of the fact that each rung on the corporate ladder has an exclusivity that is rigidly and often jealously guarded. Even in a personal situation, he should not step out of line. If his channel of communication is through his superior who reports to a vice-president, who in turn reports to the president, then this is the procedure the executive must follow. He must not assume that qualifying circumstances give him the license to bypass the procedural order and that he may approach top management directly.

When a Company Is Awarded a Juicy Contract

Of course, a congratulatory message is in order, especially if you address the letter or telegram to the man you hope will be or will continue to be your customer. Business etiquette permits such messages to be sent even to an executive not known to you personally, but with whom you hope to get involved. Good manners will require him to answer you, which establishes an entrée on an amicable basis.

One executive who was with a competing company, that had lost out on the bidding, sent a congratulatory message to the lucky bidders. It was a sporting thing to do and it made a good impression. Winning friends and encouraging goodwill even among competitors are the inherent long-term business assets which smooth the path toward congenial executive relationships.

Promotions

No human being is immune to enjoying self-gratification, nor is his pride immune to the recognition of his worth. Any status or job change should be felicitated with congratulations and good wishes. But don't make the mistake one young executive made. He sent a telegram of congratulations to a junior, whose superior, an ogre posing as a man, was transferred to another division. The junior gleefully showed the telegram to several of his associates. Its contents were circulated through the grapevine straight to top management. Management was not amused and marked the young executive as lacking in tact and good manners.

ANNIVERSARIES: BLUE AND RED LETTER DAYS

Corporate

The corporate style, whether flamboyant or restrained, is reflected in the manner in which anniversaries are celebrated. The company may be a mere stripling marking its twenty-fifth jubilee or commemorating the more prestigious centennial mile-stone. Whether or not an executive from another company is invited to attend the celebration, he need not overlook the occasion. He can send a telegram or a congratulatory letter just to let management know he rejoices with them and wishes them well.

Personnel Recognition

Most companies have some degree of paternalistic attitude toward members of their corporate families. It is not unusual to mark the tenth, the fifteenth, and the twenty-fifth anniversaries of a man's tenure in office with a celebration, and perhaps a suitable gift, such as a silver or gold pin, desk appointments, or a watch. Often the members of his department will make a collection for an additional presentation. All of this is good company relations, but what counts most is the human equation. Even if an executive has made a monetary contribution toward the departmental gift, and his name is signed on the card along with the rest of the gang, he might also mark the occasion with a warm personal touch of his own.

Engagements, Weddings, Births

Family situations, wittingly or unwittingly, infringe upon the life of the corporation. This is particularly true in suburbia and exurbia, and especially in company towns, where the social and business life are closely knit.

An announcement of an engagement, a wedding, or a birth should be acknowledged with a congratulatory letter, card, or if the relationship is a close one, with an appropriate gift.

Similar announcements received from customers, distributors, or friends of the corporation should be treated with the same courtesy and consideration.

Wedding Invitations

No executive with business savvy can afford to ignore an invitation to a wedding from a superior, a peer, or a customer. It goes without saying that unless he is out of town, he should accept all invitations to the weddings of employees reporting to him.

Generally, if you are invited only to the church services, you do not need to send a gift. If you are invited to the reception, a gift is in order.

Nevertheless, if you want to win friends and influence people, or if it is a case of *noblesse oblige,* you can send a gift even when you are not invited to the reception.

Acknowledgments

Letters, telegrams, and token of concern should be acknowledged as promptly as possible.

If, for a good, compelling reason, you are late with your acknowledgment, you can try to explain or apologize, and still express your thanks. One high-ranking official, whose new responsibilities prevented him from coping with his congratulatory messages when they arrived, sent each person a belated note reading: "Your warmhearted congratulations merited an earlier reply, but as you can appreciate, added duties and responsibilities forced me to postpone acknowledging your welcome words until today. But I am not too busy to remember your kind thoughts. Be assured that I deeply appreciate your good wishes." As in all business correspondence, typed acknowledgments are permissible, although handwritten notes are preferable.

In the case of a corporate event, such as the company anniversary, some managements assign a batch of thank-you cards to each executive to send to his customers or business friends. He may sign his name and sometimes add a word or two to personalize the acknowledgment.

IN TIMES OF CRISIS

Illness

When a member of your corporate family is ill and confined to his home or hospital, some expression of good cheer and encouragement should be sent. This also applies to active and potential customers, as well as to any person with whom you have a close business contact.

Cards are always welcome and, to give extra consideration, you can sent them at regular intervals.

If flowers are sent to the hospital, it is advisable to select a plant that is easy to care for or an arrangement in a container. Because of the shortage of nurses, some flower shops use either everlasting or artificial flowers, which they fashion into attractive, colorful designs. They require no watering and can be taken home.

In the Event of a Corporate Disaster

When a corporation suffers a disaster or goes through a crisis, any sign of friendship and concern from managements of other companies helps ease anxiety and serves as a reminder of goodwill.

If the two companies are on speaking terms, it is assumed that your president will send a telegram or a letter to the head of the corporation. Such messages are often posted on the bulletin board of the recipient company. If you feel that the situation affects the executives whom you know or have dealt with, it is a good idea either to telephone or to write a short note expressing your concern and your hope for a turn of events for the better.

When a Member of Management in Another Company Dies

When an important executive of a company or one with whom you have conducted business dies, you will wish to convey your sympathy.

Letters of condolence are generally handwritten but the typewritten letter is acceptable in business. A telegram may be sent in place of a letter. It is preferable for the young executive to send such messages to the person's immediate superior or to the next of "business kin."

If the deceased was a customer or a valued friend, condolences to the family are also in order.

Death Within Your Own Corporation

When a member of your own management or one of your subordinates dies, you are expected to pay your respects to his family. Depending on the specific arrangements, you can attend the services either at the church or at the funeral chapel. If not, you may call at the chapel to express your sympathy in person and to sign the callers' register, which is usually provided at the door. A telephone call to the church or the funeral home will, as a rule, give you the hours when the family is present.

Whether you go to the cemetery depends on the wishes of the family, your closeness to the deceased, and the custom established in your company. If he was your close superior, peer, or one of your subordinates, you will be expected to go to the cemetery, and you may also be invited to the family's home after the funeral.

Although sending flower arrangements to the funeral chapel is traditional, there are cases when, for religious or other reasons, flowers are not suitable. Hence, tactful inquiries should be made before they are sent. Frequently, the obituary notice states, "Please omit flowers," which, of course, must be scrupulously observed.

However, if flowers are acceptable, you may personally wish to send a spray, a wreath, or a basket. If the person was not in your direct line of authority, you may wish to participate in a group contribution for a flower blanket or a spray. The individual tribute depends on your business as well as your personal relationship to the deceased.

Whether it is an individual or a group tribute, the attached card can read simply, "With deepest sympathy," and be signed by one or all concerned.

At some Roman Catholic funerals flowers my not be taken into the church, and only the family's spray and altar arrangement are permitted. Similarly, at some Protestant funerals, at the request of the family, the casket may have only one flower arrangement, that of the family. In such cases, all other flowers are arranged on the funeral car attending the hearse.

Flowers are never sent to an Orthodox Jewish funeral, and are not always acceptable at either a Conservative or a Reform Jewish funeral.

Obituary notices sometimes give the name of the charitable organization to which donations may be sent in lieu of flowers. Otherwise, such donations may be sent to any research or philanthropic organization. The family is notified by the recipient without any mention of the amount, while the donor receives an acknowledgment with the amount specified for a tax deduction.

If the family is Roman Catholic, you can send a Mass card arranging for one or more services. The church has cards which should be given or sent to the family before the funeral. Similarly, arrangements can be made at the Greek Orthodox Church for periodic memorial services for a specified period of time.

Orthodox Jewish families observe the shivah, the seven-day

mourning period, when neighbors and friends attend to the cooking and feeding of the family so that they are not distracted from "the contemplation of life and death." At the time, baskets of fruit or other delicacies may be sent to the family.

Memorial Services

If the person dies in a foreign country, a distant city, or on the high seas, a memorial service is held in the community where the deceased lived and worked. The customary procedure is the same as at a funeral.

Acknowledgments

Acknowledgment of flowers, Mass cards, and donations to charity should be sent within a reasonable time. A simple, short note, preferably handwritten, need not say more than "Your kind expression of sympathy was most comforting and is deeply appreciated."

Of late, printed and engraved acknowledgments have come more and more into general use. These are supplied by funeral homes, though many families prefer to have their own cards especially printed.

20. Company Christmas Celebrations

THE COMPANY CHRISTMAS PARTY

Company Christmas parties may be on the decline, but they haven't quite lost their sparkle, and the custom is far from dying out. This is especially true of businesses that are still managed by the founder's family, where the custom may have been started by the grandfather, in some cases as long ago as the turn of the century when the company was small and intimate. The younger members of the family feel that they must cling to the tradition and fete the employees and their children. The attendance at these has been growing steadily to inflationary proportions, and where it will end, nobody knows!

At present, a good many companies prefer to concentrate on parties for younger children rather than for employees. Last year in Akron, Ohio, a suitably decorated company gymnasium accommodated thirty thousand employees' children, who were treated to cartoon shows, prizes, and candy. The parents, of course, were also present to keep an eye on their offspring, and, doubtless, to guard against any juvenile misdemeanors that might reflect unfavorably on the parents.

Another company had to borrow the local high-school gym for five thousand children and their employee parents. In one year this corporation distributed 24,000 toys at Christmas parties in their various branches.

In Denver, a family-owned business starts making plans for its Christmas festivities in the early summer. The blueprint is designed for the entertainment of about five thousand children of employees based in the home office, with the same procedure recommended to the branch plants in other parts of the country. Last year an hour-long circus show was provided in a coliseum, including refreshments and a suitable gift for each child. The widow of the founder of the company keeps an exhaustive file on every child of every employee for the companys "Santa Claus Shop."

Company Christmas parties arranged for the young children of employees are often looked upon as something for the parents to endure and for the children to enjoy. But these parties should not be taken too much for granted, or treated as just another corporate routine. The child's conduct is a reflection of the parent's standard of courtesy and good breeding.

Hence, you should give your children a thorough briefing ahead of time. You might explain to them why it is important to have them put their best foot forward. If they are old enough to go to the party, they are old enough to understand. Impress on them that this is no ordinary party and that they are official representatives at Dad's company Christmas "meeting."

To get your idea over, you might wish to give each child a title for this occasion. You can make the oldest boy Dad's assistant account executive or Dad's executive VP. A little girl is more likely to behave if she is made Dad's executive secretary or vice-president in charge of good manners.

Of course, you are up against the old dilemma. If your child behaves too well, he will be tormented by the other children as a namby-pamby. But, if he is a natural-born hellion, parents can only say a prayer, light a candle, and keep their fingers crossed—all unnecessary devices if the boy has continuous indoctrination in manners and, specifically, in "company" manners.

The briefing should include the greeting of the hosts and the thank you for the presents and for the "wonderful party." However, the most important aspect of the children's conduct is their ability to get on with the other children without becoming too self-indulgent, obstreperous, and antisocial. Some children are more difficult than others to train to be perfect specimens of the human race, but so are all adult mortals, including executives. Perhaps the difference in most cases is that because of their youth, children are more pliable and shed their antisocial habits more easily.

If the children are old enough to write or print, they might be encouraged to write a letter of thanks to the president or whoever officiated at the party. If they are too young, the parents should write the note and, perhaps, add the children's drawn "signatures."

OFFICE CHRISTMAS PARTIES

The Employee Party

Experience and a good memory make some top managers shudder at the thought: What—another office Christmas party! But inevitably, there is a group of convivial spirits who cannot bear the idea of not greeting Saint Nick with an overflow of Christmas cheer, spiked, of course, with Bacchus' special-style brew.

This is particularly prevalent in suburban and exurban areas, and in company towns, where it is more difficult to separate the social from the business life.

The tone and extent of the festivities vary with each company. Generally, the procedure is as follows: A count is taken on whether the employees want a Christmas party. Usually, the majority say "yes," and management has to bow to the inevitable. A committee is then elected, frequently drawn from the group of those individuals who voted for the party in the first place.

Sometimes management foots the entire bill and, at other times, it contributes a good share toward the expenses. Some companies, however, have a hands-off policy. It then becomes strictly an employees' party.

Although at one time many Christmas parties were restricted to employees only, the trend is to invite the wives, and many companies now include business friends.

Since Christmas Eve is reserved for those who like to decorate their own trees at home, company Christmas parties are given at any time during December. They range anywhere from cocktails or buffet supper to a supper dance with entertainment.

The old bugaboo about drinking is no light matter. You

and your wife may swear on a stack of Bibles that you'll both go easy on the liquor, but one drink invites another, and so it goes. You might keep an underlined thought in your mind that management is present and that there is always a sharp-eyed officer around who is measuring executive capacity and executive behavior, and also whether the executive's wife measures up.

If you are on the committee and the party is held on company premises, it is the responsibility of your committee to arrange to have the place cleaned up the day after. The trimmings and the decorations may remain until the New Year, but the debris and the mess should be cleared away.

If you are not on the committee, you might like to round up some signatures to thank members of the committee for their effort and congratulate them on their success. The note can be posted on the bulletin board or circulated to all the members of the committee. This should not prevent individual guests from telephoning or writing the chairman or other members to thank them and to compliment them.

The President's Christmas Party

In company towns, or in the smaller family-owned businesses, the president of the company often gives a Christmas party for the managerial staff of the company. Formerly, such parties were apt to be held in the president's home, but with the expansion of the management ranks there is a growing tendency to hold them in town or country clubs, restaurants, or hotels.

Usually the executives are invited with their wives. In a sense, this is a command performance, and it is the better part of wisdom for both to accept unless prevented by illness or a serious crisis. It is a good idea to inquire about dress. If the answer is "Don't dress," it doesn't mean that you can come in slacks and a sport jacket. Your best town suit is the answer. The same applies to your wife. The women's fashion for undressing doesn't match your executive status. Your wife will be more comfortable in a cover-up costume than in one of those see-through outfits of the fashion designers.

If you must be the life of the party, keep within the limits of good taste; otherwise you may prove to be the "knife" of the party. "In-company jokes" are just as risky as off-color stories, and the less ventured in that direction, the less the peril.

Ration your drinks, and give your wife the eye if she's overdoing it. If you are not a drinker, you cannot afford to be a spoilsport and refuse one when it is offered to you. A sober mien in an atmosphere of conviviality is not comfortable. Keep a highball in hand, with plenty of ice and water, and sip cautiously. You'll give the appearance of participating without running any risk of getting inebriated or becoming antisocial.

Since a party of this kind is not only social but also "political," it will stand you in good stead to be the perfect guest, to carry an air of pleasurable lightness, and to relate to others in a chameleonic fashion. Whenever you are with top management in an informal setting, remember to make the most of it. This, too, is long-range planning.

Time yourself. Do not leave too early. But if you must leave before the others, because you have a baby-sitter problem or whatever, do so unobtrusively. Say good night and thank your host and hostess when you can get their attention without letting the other guests in on your departure. By the same token, don't overstay your welcome. When the guests are beginning to thin out, it's time for you to say your adieus. It is better not to be among the late stragglers.

You may not need to remind your wife to send a thankyou note, which is preferable to a telephone call. But if she forgets, be sure to mention it.

COMPANY CHRISTMAS GIFTS

Instead of sponsoring Christmas parties, some companies prefer to play Santa Claus by giving each employee a token Christmas gift. In many companies it has been a tradition for a number of years. As the president of a corporation in Atlanta, each of whose 6,600 employees receives a ham, explained: "It's one of those things that if you quit doing, you get a reaction—in other words, you can't stop."

Business Week reports that probably the most common Christmas gift to employees is the turkey. One illustration the magazine cites is the tradition introduced at the turn of the century by the founder of a corporation in Chicago. Every year before Christmas he went to Indiana to shoot gobblers for each of his six employees. He stipulated in his will that the tradition be carried on. The employee roster now numbers in the thousands. The turkey-giving is maintained, though no one seems to undertake the responsibility for the safari.

Another company in Cincinnati, which used to give live turkeys, had to stop the practice because the birds often got away before the employee reached home. Now the company sends baskets of fruit and other delicacies.

Behavioral scientists and management consultants are encouraging companies to give a second thought to Christmas gifts, contending that "anything that employees *expect* to receive routinely loses its meaning."

Remember that if you are the recipient of a company Christmas present, a letter of thanks is indicated.

BUSINESS GIFTS

Customers and Friends of the Corporation

Christmas is the safest excuse for an executive to send a customer, a would-be customer, or a friend of the corporation a gift without its appearing to be a bribe, payola, or carrying with it any other nasty innuendo.

Unfortunately, some companies confuse a Christmas present, which is a personal expression of goodwill, with their own products masquerading as a gift. Such "promotion" gifts need to be reserved as samples and should be sent during the year, not at Christmas time.

Etiquette in business gift-giving is ambivalent and vexatious. It should be a personal expression, and at the same time the gift must be on the impersonal side.

The designing, manufacturing, and promoting of executive gifts is big business. Designers start in January to sweat their brains and talents to create suitable gifts, within every price range. These are selected to be meaningful, but above all impersonal.

Almost all department stores and men's specialty shops have executive gift departments, and in many cases, employ knowledgeable and experienced gift counselors to assist those executives who are bewildered or indecisive. These counselors can whip through your list of requirements and prepare a complete selection for you to choose from. There is no wear and tear of trudging through miles of aisles, eyeing a confusion of merchandise that may have no relation whatsoever to your requirements.

For armchair shoppers there are mail-order firms that have such specialties as fruit-of-the-month, cheese-of-the-month, and flowers-of-the-month—tasteful reminders at regular intervals that there is an executive or a sales manager who cares about his customers and his friends.

Too many companies send liquor, champagne, or wine, and let it go at that. This is not always advisable. One has to take into account drinking taboos, religious restrictions, and particular tastes, where a case of wine may not be half as much appreciated as one good bottle of aged Armagnac. Only if you know the man well, and know his tastes or his convictions about liquor, should you risk sending him any alcoholic beverages.

Your Christmas Gift List

You cannot afford to leave this to the last minute and then get up a haphazard list of those you think ought to get a company gift, and hope to heaven you haven't left anyone out.

When you make up your list, give it your most careful planning and checking. Make sure you keep a copy safely filed away for next year's checking.

If you are sending a gift to an executive who has an assistant with whom you have also been dealing, by all means include him.

Don't overlook the customer from whom you haven't had any business this year. If he had received gifts from you in previous years, it is bad business etiquette to neglect him this year. Besides, a little remembrance from you might serve as a gentle nudge.

The Company That Forbids Gifts

When it comes to receiving gifts, some companies take their cue from Washington. They regard gift-giving, even at Christmas time, with suspicion and disfavor. They forbid all their employees to accept gifts of any kind from any individual or company with whom they do business.

Such companies usually send letters to their suppliers and sales offices stating their policy.

It is axiomatic that every executive is obliged to respect and honor such requests. Circumventing the company ruling by sending a gift to an employee's home would be an embarrassment to the recipient and a discourtesy to the company.

Intraoffice Giving

Christmas offers an appropriate occasion for an executive to express his personal thanks gracefully and appreciatively to those who have worked closely with him during the year.

(1) *Your secretary* is a must. You may be wise to discuss this subject with your wife. Your secretary's present should be carefully thought out and selected. It might be something personal, such as a handbag, a designer-signed scarf, a piece of jewelry, or perhaps a government savings bond. But, please, nothing that she can use on her desk or that would remind her of being a working girl.

It is courteous if, along with your signature on the card, your wife adds hers as well. Your secretary and your wife may never have met in person, but they are certainly "telephone pals." Also, there must have been times when your secretary did personal errands for you that relieved your wife of the chore. Your secretary will be pleased to know that your wife too appreciates her helpfulness.

(2) *Your immediate subordinates*. Since you work closely with each man, you ought to have some knowledge of his tastes, his hobbies, his interests. It might be records, books, ties, in fact anything that is personal but not necessarily something that relates to his work.

(3) *The switchboard operator and the receptionist*. Modest presents are in order, but don't settle on boxes of candy.

That might be suitable for outsiders, who do not know the girls, but wish to thank them for past courtesies. Your secretary should be helpful, or you might ask your wife. Any gift, however modest, should be meaningful and show that some thought has been given to the pleasure of the recipient.

(4) *Christmas gifts you receive.* When you write your letter of thanks, it is a good idea to mention the gift and your personal enjoyment in the use of it. If your acknowledgment is being sent to someone within your own organization, the letter is written on your personal stationery; acknowledgments for gifts from other companies are written on company stationery and addressed to the individual who signed the card.

CHRISTMAS CARDS

The sending of Christmas cards, like Topsy, has "growed and growed" until its true meaning and significance have been distorted into a burden.

Some corporations have established the policy of no Christmas cards. Instead, a contribution is made in the name of the corporation to a charitable organization listing all the companies and persons to whom Christmas cards would normally have been sent. Each person listed is notified of this action by the charitable organization without mentioning the amount of the donation. The corporation, of course, receives an acknowledgment from the organization for tax purposes.

Yet, there are still many companies that observe the traditional exchange of cards, especially those with extensive lists of customers, distributors, and foreign affiliates. Usually these cards are designed and printed to reflect the company's image. Each executive is given a supply to address to those persons with whom he has a business relationship.

An executive should be selective in building up his Christmas card list. Once you have someone on your list, it is inadvisable to remove him, even though he hasn't bought anything from you for years.

Company Christmas cards are usually sent to the office address. However, if the executive has had a close business relationship with the individual and has met his wife, it is courteous to address the card to both and send it to their home.

Exchanging personal Christmas cards with associates in the office depends on the attitude of the particular company. Some companies encourage it, others frown upon it. Nevertheless, you will probably want to send your personal Christmas card to the home address of your boss, perhaps to your immediate subordinates, to your secretary, and to some of your colleagues.

21. The International Scene

With United States business turning the world into a global marketplace, a new breed of executives is emerging—the "globocrat." Staff members with American production expertise and management know-how are not traveling as much as they are commuting to regions that years ago would have been inconceivable as possible industrial centers.

For the American globocrat it's a two-way lane. While he is indoctrinating the natives in American neotechniques and Yankee efficiency, he must be receptive to differences in culture, manners, and in some countries, to vast differences in religious observances, all of which are sensitive areas that must be treated with the utmost seriousness. The American globocrat dealing with foreign executives, and in many cases, with native workers, must include as part of his traveling equipment the patience of a saint, the wisdom of a philosopher, and the open-mindedness to accept and appreciate the customs and mores that appear alien to him and unrelated to his American way of life.

What that "little guy" did or said in Pakistan, Japan, Botswana, or Argentina may do for amusing anecdotes at cocktail parties back in the States, but like the "Go home, Yankee" graffiti, it is not funny in the lexicon of international understanding and global business.

Dealing with Latins who are conditioned to a *mañana* attitude, and to whom promises and clocks are both inventions of the devil, is enough to drive an uninitiated American executive to counting "worry beads," a custom Greek and Arab gentlemen enjoy, but not for the same reason.

Native workers in such far-flung areas as the Philippines, Korea, Taiwan, North Africa, and South America have a telepathic pact on how to torment the Yanks without really trying. An American engineer will explain exactly what is wrong with a certain machine and how it can be corrected. The American must not commit the indiscretion of touching the machine or making the simple adjustment himself. The native worker will smile and say what sounds like "Yes, sir. I see." The next day the adjustment has not been made, and once again the engineer goes through the same routine, with the native worker still smiling, and still saying, "Yes, sir. I see." And so it goes on and on until the adjustment through some form of osmosis is finally made, or the machine breaks down completely.

Even when there is no language barrier and the American is thoroughly conversant with the language of the country in which he finds himself, he still may not be speaking the same ethnic or cultural dialect, whether he is addressing top management or the native workers.

There is the American agricultural expert who arrived in India full of do-good idealism and the American-style efficiency, only to find himself frustrated and in the end thoroughly disillusioned. Where did he fail? He neglected to take into account age-old local methods, folklore, customs, and superstitions. The natives were polite but resistant, perhaps not so much to the changes as to the American's eagerness to cut right through primitive practices to achieve speedy, efficient results. He returned to the United States feeling misunderstood, his dedicated sense of service misconstrued as American aggression. But what really rankled was that he knew he was regarded as gauche by the punctiliously polite Indians, because he had persistently tried to get things done, and done properly.

Americans abroad should cultivate the art of listening intuitively and with sensitivity before they commit the common error of listening to themselves and then sounding off.

YOUR PASSPORT TO SUCCESS

Here are a few items you might wish to include in your baggage, and which might prove to be open sesames to help you bridge cultural, ethnic, and language gaps.

Your Business Card

In addition to your regular card in English, have business cards printed in the language of the country you expect to be in. Or you may use one card with the necessary information in both languages printed on each side. This is a flattering courtesy which will not go unnoticed or be unappreciated.

Titles

Titles are important. In Asia, the Middle East, and in many European countries, the managing director is the top man. "President" is usually an honorary title bestowed upon a member of the founding or related family, who is often no more than a figurehead. Whatever your American title may be, make yourself a managing director, and you'll be in.

It is also well to remember that the corporate structure in most of these areas is vertical, where rank and position, as well as caste, are highly esteemed. It is not unusual to find a subordinate in a foreign country, in the presence of a higher-echelon official, if not actually clicking his heels, at least standing in the posture of respectful attention until his superior recognizes his presence.

An American globocrat may have been on the friendliest terms with an executive of comparable status in the country he is visiting (he might even have entertained him lavishly in the United States), but the visitor cannot expect any overtures from the foreign national until the local managing director has made the first move. Once the visitor has been invited by the managing director for lunch or dinner, some of the other staff members may follow suit.

In the Scandinavian countries, in Germany, as well as in the Low Countries, officials of a company are frequently addressed by their titles, such as "Herr Director" or "Herr Engineer," both in speech and in writing. In Germany especially, college degrees are cherished, and it is not unusual to hear a layman referred to as "Herr Doktor." When in doubt, some American businessmen have been known to bypass the titles and use the simple form of "Mister," or the native equivalent, without stirring up any international tensions. Apparently we are doing something right, since northern Europeans do not indulge in the love-hate syndrome that is so manifest in relation to Americans in other countries.

Business Correspondence

If the multinational corporation does not have an affiliate office in the country where the globocrat is scheduled to be, a good safeguard is for him to take along a reasonable supply of his business stationery, especially envelopes bearing his return address.

Foreign business correspondence, whether written in English or the language of the country, is much more flowery, with the rhetoric bordering on the extravagant. The short, business-like, American-type letter may sound curt and might even be interpreted as ungracious in countries where, no matter how great the pressures, there is always time for courtesy.

Like the East Indians, the Latins, and particularly the French, will conclude a letter with an elaborate salutation, such as one received by a globocrat that ended with these words: "I humbly implore you, dear sir, to believe in my sincerest greetings and my highest hopes for our continued friendly relations and our closer affiliation for the ever-increasing betterment of our mutual concerns."

He may have to be his own secretary and drop his letters in a convenient mailbox, if he wants to be sure his correspondence does not end up in a trash can. Bellboys, concierges, and some clerks in foreign hotels have a penchant for "collecting" uncancelled stamps.

In the Soviet Union, as in all of her satellite countries, even airmail letters may reach their destinations after some delay. In the Middle East arena, where tensions run high, nervous bureaucrats deny that letters are being opened. Nevertheless, a Beirut English-language newspaper carried an editorial complaining about censorship of the mail.

British postal service is good. Respect for the privacy of correspondence seems to be indigenous to the English character.

French postal service also functions very well. Regular mail is delivered three times a day, and the *pneumatique* is still in operation, reaching any destination in Paris in less than two hours.

Most European countries are quite aware of the American slogan, "Time is money." Still, it would pay the American businessman to check with his local branch office or with concierge at his hotel on the local efficiency of the mail and the telegraph service to avoid the embarrassment of a vice president of an American corporation about to venture into large investments in Europe. En route he was detained in Spain. On his arrival in London he found that his tentative acceptance of an invitation for a luncheon meeting of the top management of a British company had not been cancelled, and the officers of the British corporation had waited for the American guest of honor for over an hour. His cable finally arrived in the British office of the president—three days later. His only excuse was his total ignorance of the fact that some of the Spanish cable service was still running on a nineteenth-century time table.

INTERNATIONALLY SPEAKING

Americans are lazy linguists. For years they were smugly secure in the belief that the American tourist dollar was sufficient to serve them eloquently in any language. They were further encouraged in their insulation by the fact that so many Europeans are fantastic linguists, fluent in several languages, including English. Also, not to be overlooked, was the imprint Mother England left upon her colonies in varied parts of the world during her Empire glory-days. Children, before they learned to read or write, were able to chatter in English, as well as in their native tongue.

Recently, an American newly arrived in Tangier lost his way in the labyrinth of alleys, lanes, and streets. He approached two little Arab boys who were jabbering away in French. In his best college French, he asked the boys for directions, only to have them stare at him with their beautiful limpid eyes, until one little fellow spoke up: "Sir, you speak terrible French." Then in perfect English, he gave the American the directions he required.

Most Moroccans are multilingual, speaking Arabic, French, Spanish, and English. Tangier has a polyglot language all its own called "Tangerine." Practically every sentence contains French, Spanish, and Arabic words.

Almost every major capital in the world now has street signs or other public notices printed in four or five languages, such as English, French, German, Italian, and Spanish. In Vienna, policemen wear armbands indicating the language they speak.

Little Belgium is also getting into the big-league language act, though her bilingual ambivalence between her French and Flemish factions continues to plague the citizenry. Everything, even streets, have two names, one in Flemish and one in French. Since now both NATO and the Common Market have established headquarters in Brussels, it is one of the few world capitals with three different sets of foreign ambassadors, one accredited to Belgium itself, another to the European communities, and still another to NATO. Belgium has a lenient tax-free policy which has encouraged American industry to establish subsidiary companies there. Within the past ten years investments have totalled over $780 million.

In the Scandinavian countries English is called "the language of commerce" and, in fact, is regarded as the second language, which is taught in all the schools from elementary to college. The Swedes, Danes, and Norwegians are unusually gifted linguists, and are at home in German and French; some are quite likely to be equally conversant with Spanish and Italian. They also speak a dialect called "Skandavisk," which is an amalgam of all the northern idioms, and if an American globocrat can master that, he's in business.

Japan, where the modernization process has propelled the country out of its shogun-controlled isolationism into one of the world's great industrial nations, is encouraging the teaching of English in its schools.

However, the average citizen in Tokyo, even when he is wearing a Westernized business suit, finds difficulty in coping with the Western languages. He has trouble with the pronunciation of such letters as *l*, *th*, and *v*.

And though legend has it that the Japanese originally descended from the Chinese, it is curious that the Chinese have no letter *r* and pronounce it in foreign words as *l*, whereas the Japanese have no letter *l* and always pronouce *l* as *r*.

The language barrier does not affect the Japanese businessman's innate courtesy, and he is always willing to be of service to a stranger. If you ask directions, even in sign language, the reply may be "Hai. Hai." This means either yes or no. Actually, it is an acknowledgment that the Japanese gentleman is willing to listen, rather than that he understands what you are trying to say.

Tokyo streets are not numbered and even local residents lose their way. An American globocrat venturing out into the streets of Tokyo without an interpreter or guide should carry a map of the city, and also have the names and addresses of the places he is going to written out for him in Japanese characters. This may help postpone an incipient nervous breakdown, for, unlike other Asians, the Japanese are punctilious about appointments.

The American might also take into account that traffic in Tokyo is more horrendous than in New York, Rome, or Paris. Taxicab drivers are called kamikazes, but even their suicidal antics cannot rescue one from a Tokyo-style traffic jam.

Also good to remember is that the twenty-fifty of each month is usually payday for most Tokyo employees. On that day, traffic moves at a snail's pace, restaurants and nightclubs are jammed, and even the kamikazes get lost.

In Israel the linguistic problem is simply defined. It is referred to as a country where they read Hebrew, write English, and speak Yiddish. "Shalom" is the universal greeting. It means peace, and is used interchangeably for "hello" and "good-bye."

This is not to be confused with the Islamic salutation used throughout the Arab countries, which is generally "As-Salam mu Alaikum." The return greeting is usually "Wa-Alaikum mussalam." Muhammadans conclude all meetings, social or otherwise, with a blessing: "Maa-Is-Salamah," meaning "Peace be with you."

Latin America, from the Rio Grande to Cape Horn, including the Caribbean Islands, is split into four main languages: Spanish in eighteen countries, Portuguese in Brazil, Creole in Haiti, and English on many Caribbean islands.

You may do very well with your high-school Spanish in the Caribbean area, but you may find that certain words and phrases have an entirely different meaning in the southern part of South America. Spanish is understood by many Brazilians, but few Spanish-speaking people understand Portuguese. As for the musical, lilting Creole language, even Frenchmen need a score to understand the idiom.

Buoyed by a booming worldwide economy, many foreign businessmen are studying English. If an American globocrat hasn't the time or the inclination to return the compliment by studying the language of the country he has to visit, he will ease international relations considerably if he learns and uses the few basic words that speak the language of courtesy in every part of the world, such as "please," "thank you," "good morning," and "good evening."

Of course, suggesting that he take along a dictionary of customary words and phrases, which comes in a pocket-size edition, is equivalent to reminding him to take along a toothbrush.

YOUR BUSINESS HOSTS ABROAD

Business Is Not First in Other Countries

In most foreign countries business is seldom if ever discussed during lunch, dinner, or tea or coffee breaks. Frequently, no business is initiated until some form of refreshments has been offered.

In Japan every meeting in the office or elsewhere is conducted with formal ceremony. Tea and cakes are served and the social amenities exchanged before anyone presumes to deal with the affairs of the day.

In the Middle East and northern Africa a businessman is incapable of any discussion until his visitor has joined him in an Arabian-version coffee break—with very black, very pungent, overly sweet coffee or mint tea. Refusing to partake of this hospitable gesture is a social blunder. Incidentally, mint tea is regarded as a panacea for almost all physical discomforts, especially the common tourist complaint of diarrhea. If you are not fond of mint tea, you had better not mention that you are suffering from any intestinal disorder.

In England, of course, the tea hour is sacrosanct, and may run the gamut from simple biscuits and buns to a high tea repast which may include assorted sandwiches or a hot dish plus fruit tarts and cup after cup of tea laced with milk.

Entertainment—Foreign Style

An American abroad should not feel slighted or rejected if he is not invited to dine *en famille*. In many regions there is a definite demarcation between a man's social and business activities, and his home life. Though the purdah has been lifted in many parts of Asia and North Africa, the inbred seraglio tradition prevails psychologically. This, despite the fact that more and more Islamic girls are being sent abroad to complete their college education in prominent universities in Europe and America.

In Morocco one may see fashionably dressed young women wearing the latest Paris shoes and carrying handbags, but over their stylish dresses they still wear their native jubbah. At foreign embassy parties in Marrakech, the Moroccan gentlemen still continue to come stag.

Nevertheless, the wholesale exchange of globocrats and the scrambling together in one melting pot of multifarious cultures is rapidly diverting old customs into a new and different social order.

An American executive who took his wife with him to Kuwait received an invitation for both to the palace of an oil-rich sheik for dinner. The guests consisted of eight men, plus the host, and one other woman—a beautiful Italian contessa who flirted charmingly in Italian, English, Spanish, and French. The host's wives never appeared. The guests sat on low banquettes, though as a special courtesy to the Americans and the Europeans, extra cushions were provided, which did not add to their comfort, since the table was too low. The food was brought in a massive bowl, but no knives or forks were offered. Each diner broke off a chunk from the thin bread that lined the bowl, making sure to use his right hand since Muhammadans reserve the left hand for cleansing purposes only. The bread was dipped into a rice and pine nut mixture, which was rolled into a ball, then eaten with pieces of meat plucked from the lamb that decorated the center of the bowl. The host never sat down at all, but wandered from one guest to another to be sure that his hospitality was being honored by the amount of food being consumed. Refraining from eating or refusing any dish is a social breach not accepted lightly by the host.

Alcohol is seldom if ever served in a devout Moslem household. And before you automatically put a cigar or a cigarette into your mouth, wait to get your clue from your host. If he is toying with his prayer beads, which he might be doing while he is chatting with his guests, you might realize that he does not approve of smoking, especially in his home.

While some Moslems are breaking away from the old rules, the majority still follow the Prophet's dictum: no smoking or drinking.

The Moslems also observe some of the same dietary restrictions as do the Israelis: no pork or shellfish is ever allowed.

In Israel home entertaining is frequent, and the cuisine is simple. The observance of kosher dietary rules are more strictly adhered to in restaurants and even in the cosmopolitan hotels than they are in some homes. If you are enjoying a steak dinner, requesting butter for your bread or milk for your coffee may prove embarrassing. The *kashruth* rules forbid the mixing of dairy products with meat dishes.

Smoking during the Sabbath, which starts at sundown on Friday and ends at sundown on Saturday, would be a blunder not accepted too tolerantly.

In Japan wives are not included in business entertainment and even mistresses are excluded from such functions. Mistress tradition in Japan dates back to the ninth century, and most present-day executives continue to enjoy this social freedom without any of the accompanying Western stigma. Mistresses are, in fact, status symbols. It is not unusual for a businessman's credit to be rated on the style in which he maintains his *nigo*.

Geisha girls are professionally trained singers and dancers, and their sole function is to be charming and entertaining in a highly stylized way. Occasionally, they take over as waitresses. To assume that a geisha is a call girl would be interpreted as a gross indiscretion.

The Japanese in their Westernizing process are rapidly discarding many of their old customs. Sitting on the floor while dining, with legs tucked under, used to be a tortuous experience for many Occidentals. Now restaurants and even homes in urban areas have their low dining tables stationed over a pit. One need only let one's legs dangle in the pit and concentrate on enjoying the dinner in comfort. The more modern restaurants now have both tables and pits.

One tradition the Japanese have retained is the removal of shoes before crossing the threshold. This still applies to all homes and to some business establishments. However, the larger business and industrial concerns, particularly those in the big cities, have shelved, together with the kimono and the low bowing, the custom of removing shoes in their buildings.

In some organizations slippers are supplied in the anteroom. This should give you a clue. Nevertheless, it is a good idea, especially in the hinterland, to ask if the shoes should be removed or to follow the example of your Japanese hosts.

If you are planning a trip to Japan, take an inventory of your socks. A protruding exposed toe or a raveled heel is not only embarrassing to you, but is a poor, no-confidence-inspiring image for an aspiring executive.

In India the hospitality is warm and friendly; an invitation to a home can be an interesting experience. Many of the old traditions are still maintained, and a ceremonial dinner can be exotic, provided, of course, one has an educated palate for hot curries and spices. The important food taboo to remember is that cows are regarded as sacred and are never slaughtered for human consumption. If you are a steak-and-potato man, forget it while you are in India.

Wives usually participate in business-social occasions. In their beautiful colorful saris, their function is purely decorative. Even a highly educated, well-traveled and experienced woman will remain silent and in the background, giving her husband the honor of demonstrating that he is master in his own home.

In Germany as well as in the Netherlands, gemutlichkeit reigns, and visiting globocrats get the open-house treatment. Weight-watchers and diet-faddists may find the going tough, since dinners are usually three-hour-long hearty affairs, and the *hausfrau's* métier is to urge more and more food as a sign of her hospitality. She takes pride in her *Sauerbraten mit Kartoffelklosse*, to say nothing of a luscious selection of three or four different home-baked cakes and tarts.

A Frenchman rarely invites a stranger to his home. Usually he and his wife entertain the visitor in a restaurant that has achieved a reputation for haute cuisine. The ordering of the food and wine is ceremonious, involving the host in lengthy discussions and inquiries with the maître d', the waiter, and the sommelier. The guest's role is to sit by quietly and accept with gracious enthusiasm each dish that is served, which may not necessarily be of his own choosing. The same applies to the wine, which should be sipped appreciatively, not gulped down like water. Smoking between courses, even at a simple dinner, will mark you as a primitive with neither manners nor palate and unworthy of France's justifiably famous cuisine.

In England, as in all her remaining colonies and dominions, an American globocrat, if not exactly treated as though he were a kissin' cousin, is accepted with friendly kinship. Invitations may be extended for long weekends in the country, and, of course, dinners in town with the family.

At public dinners, there is no smoking before the Queen's toast is offered, a formality observed by all true Englishmen, regardless of what part of the world they are in.

Spanish business hours, according to American standards, are eccentric to say the least. Siesta time, dear to the life style of every Spaniard of every class and every rank, is piously observed. The siesta hours, during which all business establishments are shut down, may range from twelve noon or one o'clock until as late as four o'clock. Paterfamilias retires to his shuttered home and is incommunicado. The usual procedure is lunch with the family, followed by a refreshing nap. Stores and offices open again at four o'clock and continue to do business until eight. After that, executives can be found at a café sipping a drink and discussing life, love, happiness, and occasionally business. Spanish wives are never present at such gatherings. They are normally stag. The dinner, whether in the home or in restaurants, starts at about ten o'clock.

At one time most Latin countries held the siesta hours sacred, but the trend now is toward a work day of 9 to 6, with a one- or, as in Italy, two-hour lunch period. While in the provinces the French are still likely to take a siesta, the larger cities are fast abandoning this pleasant leisurely custom.

In almost all the countries of South America, the bigger cities have switched to the North American work schedule. Throughout Chile, the one-hour lunch is fast becoming the rule. In Brazil, Colombia, and Ecuador the business hours match ours. The Brazilians dine at 7:30 or so, but in the summer the cocktail hour can stretch to 9 o'clock or later.

The large corporations in the big cities in Argentina have dropped the siesta observance, but many of the smaller business concerns and those located in the interior continue to take two or three hours rest in midafternoon, particularly in the warm season.

Peru is one country which still follows the old Spanish siesta tradition. Most business and commercial houses open at

8 A.M. and close at 1 P.M. for the siesta. They reopen at 4 P.M. and close again at 8 P.M. The banks, however, are open only from 8 A.M. until 12:30 P.M.

RELIGIOUS OBSERVANCES

An experienced globocrat always keeps his antenna sensitively tuned to the religious observances of the country he is visiting, or in which he is stationed. One minor misstep might be a booby trap that will blow up into a major *cause célébre*.

Islamic Countries

Ramadan, the thirty-day fast period, should be taken into account, especially by those globocrats who are on a tight schedule. This is the most rigidly observed religious holiday, when Moslems fast each day, refraining from food and drink between dawn and dark. The day is usually spent in prayer and meditation, but many persons are too limp to do more than just sleep. Trade and public affairs slow down with little hope for any business to be transacted until possibly late in the evening. The Islamic calendar is lunar, with Ramadan coming at different times each year. Western businessmen should synchronize their calendars in advance if they hope to achieve their goals.

Friday is the Islamic holy day, when no business is transacted. A devout Muhammadan believes that he cannot enter Paradise unless he gives alms to the beggars. It is on that day that beggars as well as lepers, are out in full force. Hence foreigners will find it the better part of discretion to remain indoors.

In North Africa there are Moslems, Christians, and Jews, which means that Friday, Saturday, and Sunday are holy days, leaving only four working days in which to conduct business.

Beirut observes two holidays a week—Friday for Moslems and Sunday for Christians.

Non-Moslems are forbidden to enter certain mosques, and, in fact, they must not be seen in the vicinity after sundown. In those mosques where visitors are welcome, shoes must be removed before entering. It is also proper to rinse your hands at the fountain or from the pitcher stationed in front of the mosque for this purpose.

Israel

In Jerusalem three sabbath days are observed: Friday for Moslems, Saturday for Jews, Sunday for Christians.

Saturday is the Jewish sabbath, when no business is conducted in Israel. Even public transportation is not available on that day. Government departments work six days, however, from Sunday to Friday. Synagogues may be visited on Saturday during services, but men must remember to wear their hats.

Asia

In most major cities throughout Asia business is conducted on Sunday, and in many of the cities the employees are given half-holidays on Saturday.

Buddhism, which is practiced in a large portion of Asia, from Ceylon to the islands of Japan, has no specific sabbath day. Shrines and temples are open every day for prayer and worship.

Most of the Buddhist and, in the case of Japan, the Shinto temples and shrines are the quintessence of Oriental beauty. Many of them are open to visitors. Shoes must be removed before entering these holy places. The Japanese usually don a pair of wool slipper-socks, since the floors of these buildings are often cold.

Italy

Blasphemy, or invoking the Lord's name in vain, is a violation of civil law in Italy. There is an active Carrie-Nationish committee called the National Union Against Blasphemy. Their commandos, numbering more than three thousand, are energetically alert, particularly in bars, nightclubs, and stadiums, apprehending sinners against God and violators against the law. The Italian courts are rigid: they will not recognize education or social status as an extenuating circumstance in blasphemy cases.

The Soviet Union

The bureaucratic red tape in the Soviet Union and the satellite countries can be a maze of prohibitions, restrictions, and incongruities that baffles Americans, inured to uninhibited speech and movement. The Bureau of Security and Consular Affairs of the U. S. Department of State has issued a brochure outlining the salient do's and don'ts for those traveling in the Soviet Union. These are also applicable to her satellite countries.

Repeated incidents notwithstanding, many an American who has gone to the Soviet Union in a business or professional capacity found a warm cooperative reception. Of course, you are well screened before you leave the U.S.—you have to state the purpose of your trip, the area of your interest, and what you wish or need to see. Accordingly, the Soviet authorities will arrange for you to be in touch with the right government agency, which in turn will set up your appointments and specify the proper contacts.

The American businessman will face in the Soviet Union a unique dichotomy—on the one side, the bureaucracy of the Communist regime with its severe, stilted rules and regulations, which are basically anti-foreign; on the other side, the people of Russia, with their inherent Slavic hospitality, their outgoing warmheartedness and their effervescence. If you can bridge the gap between these two, you will find much in the arts, the crafts and the sciences of Soviet Russia. You will also enjoy the vodka, the caviar, the balalaikas, and the plaintive Russian songs.

YOUR PERSONAL FOREIGN POLICY

The hate-America virus which is spreading to epidemic proportions in various parts of the world has infected many of our traveling executives with a severe case of guilt-edged insecurity.

A good example is the situation in Latin America, which is duplicated in other parts of the globe. As *New York Times* correspondent Ted Szulc reported, the prevailing attitude is "that everything the United States does in Latin America stems from a sinister design to maintain control over the region. Thus the United States is to be blamed for *not* aiding Latin America—the better to keep her subservient, the critics cried. But when the Alliance for Progress was launched to aid Latin America, the same critics charged that this Kennedy program was a plot to perpetuate domination by U.S. economic interests. . . . The grudging conclusion is . . . that the United States is damned if it does and damned if it does not."

To retain one's rationality in a vortex of irrationalities, one must never lose sight of the fact that is was through American enterprise, American commerce, and American foreign aid that the cornucopia has overflowed lavishly for the development and profitability of other countries.

Etiquette has no boundaries, and propriety boasts no distinct dialect. This is particularly true for corporate etiquette. It is in essence international. At its base is an acknowledgment of respect and consideration of the other person or groups of people, concern for their comfort and ease, and it is a means of softening the harsher tones of human relationships.

In his book *Voices Offstage* Marc Connelly relates an incident when he and the late Royal Prince William of Sweden were going up in the elevator of the residence of the American minister in Stockholm. Connelly at the time was the guest of honor at the reception celebrating the first performance in Sweden of his *The Green Pastures*. When the elevator stopped and the door opened automatically, the Prince stood aside for Connelly to leave first. As Connelly confessed, he knew nothing of elevator protocol, but said, "After you, Your Royal Highness." "Oh no," said Prince William, "you are a guest of my country, and you must let me be hospitable."

Connelly insisted: "Sir, at the moment we are standing on what is by international law American territory, so you are a guest of the United States."

But the Prince ignored Connelly's grandiose hand wave and told him with mock gravity: "You have made an error. The floor a foot ahead of us may be technically the United States, but we are standing in a Swedish lift directly above Swedish ground."

Eventually they solved the problem by marching out of the elevator shoulder to shoulder.

In a very real sense, every American globocrat is an ambassador representing his country. It is fitting for him to project an image of his most attractive self. He can be proud without being arrogant, and he can be generous, even lavish with his technological knowledge and his homespun know-how, but, by the same token, he should be receptive to much that he can absorb from other cultures and give homage to the splendid contributions of each country.

As a goodwill ambassador he should also help create a more favorable attitude toward his own country. He might follow Winston Churchill's philosophy: "When abroad, I never criticize the government of my country, but I make up for it when I come home."

The focal guideline for the American business and industrial globocrats may well be that, in spite of the many languages, unrelated customs, and divergent values, the world is but one small planet. Perhaps, with enough globocrats spanning it as carriers of goodwill and good business, our world will become not only an economic, but a scientific, civic, and humane uniforce.